PROJECT
WE ARE
FREE

Women With A Voice

Presented by Connextion Works

Copyright 2017 Connextion Works
All Rights Reserved

ISBN-13: 978-1976452727
ISBN-10: 1976452724

Table Of Contents

Dedication v

Introduction... 1

About Dr. Tamika A. Anderson 9
    From Fear to Freedom..................................... 11

About Henrietta Kay Fountaine - Hadley.................... 22
    Promises 24

About Kimberly McGowan 39
    Stand in Your Confidence................................. 40

About Virginia Manning 46
    The Wish 47

About Monique McGilberry 54
    Embrace Your Five-Minute Husband 55

About Marchet Denise Fullum 61
    No More Wire Hangers..................................... 63

About Kim PossABLE.. 75
    Emerging Spirit 77

About Jalila Poole - Lewis 94
    Let Freedom Reign.. 96

Conclusion... 108

Dedication

This book is lovingly dedicated to the scared little girl or boy inside of each one of us whose voice has been muted by a traumatic experience. You are not alone. May you find the strength and courage to free yourself from the trauma of your past.

Introduction

Project We Are Free was birthed as a result of my life being shaken to its core. Initially, I had this idea of what my life was going to be like and had planned my life as well as I could. My life had taken a horrific turn. It was taking a turn that didn't resemble anything in the vision that I had created for how I wanted to live my life. In a flash, I was watching my life, goals, dreams, and just about everything dissipate right before my eyes. My initial reaction was to be fearful of the unknown. I quickly realized that I needed to have fearless faith and I began to surrender my control and trust the process of my journey. I had no control of the situation, I had lost a lot, and I was still losing just about everything.

My life had turned upside down and inside out. I was homeless and living out of my car even though my name was on the mortgage of our home. Abuse is such a taboo subject in our culture and due to growing up in an abusive home as a child, I did not have the support of family. I was living in a small town with no family, friends or a support system. At the time, I didn't know that isolation is a classic tactic of an abuser. The church we attended was his home church and the pastor, his wife, and the congregation turned their back on me and ignored my requests for help. I had finally come to a point where I was tired, I was exhausted and I wanted to be free.

The last time my husband held a knife to my throat a police officer took me to the side and said look here unless you make a change the next time we come back to your home it's gonna be to take you outta here in a body bag. Don't you understand, this guy cares more about that umbrella on the floor than he does you. After that I once again found myself passed out on the floor from being strangled by my husband. This was my wake up call. My life flashed before me as I was laid out cold on the floor, I knew I needed to make a change.

The fear and pain of me staying in an abusive marriage finally became greater than the fear of leaving and venturing out into a new life of the unknown on my own free from abuse. For so long I was afraid to leave because I was afraid that I could not survive and thrive on my own. I realized that I had been asleep at the wheel of my life. This was a moment of awakening for me. I was ready to go on my spiritual journey to understand how I had allowed my life to get to such a low place.

I needed a different process because it was always about what other people had done to me and how I was the victim. Who I am is not about what I have been through but what I choose to do with it to help someone else who may be going through at dark time in their life. I had to come to understanding that I don't have to lead with the disease to please. We just can't please everyone. I had to take the time to do the work and get clear about who I was at the core of my existence. Everyday I would look into the mirror and tell myself, "I want to be like me!". It's perfectly alright for you to be like you. It's a process and a journey to get to who you are at the core. What has happened or what is happening in your life is paving the way for you. Proverbs 18:16 says, your gifts will make room for you and bring you before great men. Don't be discouraged if all hell is breaking loose in your life right now. You are right where you need to be.

I began to create a new vision for my life. As I was transitioning out of this situation I created a new vision board for myself.

Between God and my vision boards I started seeing many things in my life come to pass. I was very specific with how I wanted my life to change. I wrote and posted exactly what I wanted to manifest in my life. I even wrote specific figures that I wanted in checking account and savings account with a specific date. I didn't know the how and I wasn't concerned about it. We're not supposed to worry about the how. We're just to trust and have faith that as long as we take action and do the work, our needs will be met.

For those of you who have a business or idea inside of you that needs to be developed, don't get stuck on perfection. It's okay to have versions 1, 2, and 3. Implement whatever it is that you've been procrastinating about and regroup at a later time. Just get it done! Oftentimes, the experts don't tell you about the pain, hurt, and failures they went through to achieve the level of success and freedom that they have. The challenges you are facing right now are preparing you for something greater. Your experiences are preparing you by building your character, giving you more substance, and taking you through the fire so that you will know firsthand what it's like so that you can help someone else in the same or similar situation.

I had endured a lot of pain, suffering, loss, overwhelm, and loneliness. I didn't want other women to have to experience the type of pain and hurt that I was feeling. I wanted other women to know that no matter what they were going through, they're not alone. I wanted them to know that they didn't have to suffer in silence. Even though I wanted to help other women, I was still carrying the shame of what happened within my marriage.

I decided to record a video telling my story of surviving abuse. I wanted to help other women who were being abused and suffering in silence. I did not use my real name. I used the pseudonym IHaveAVoice100 because I was still ashamed of what I had gone through and scared that someone I knew would find out about it.

Even though I wanted to help other women I still wanted to hide. I posted the video on Twitter and Queen Latifah retweeted my video to over 6.5 Million people. Initially, I was excited and then my heart sank. I got nervous about my worst fear. Shortly after she retweeted the video, a few people contacted me to ask if it was me on Queen Latifah's feed. Panic set in, my cover was blown, and I had to make a choice. Either continue hiding or get out there and share my message.

Someone asked me why I was not using my real name. I explained why and she urged me to use my real name and share my message of survival with the world. I took a deep breath and mustered up the courage to no longer care about what people thought about me. My focus was going to be on helping other women free themselves from whatever was holding them back.

I just want to tell you that no matter what you are going through right now, it is preparing you for something greater. I like to say it's building my faith muscle. DO NOT be afraid to share your story! You never know who is watching, listening, and ready to support you and your mission, movement, message. Whether you know it or not, some of the most unlikely people do watch with positive intentions.

All I can say is, had I not gone through what I have been through, I would not have met some of the most AMAZING people along my journey of healing. I would not be out here helping other women in this capacity. I am thankful for the people who have stuck by me through the pain and tears. I am forever grateful!

Don't be afraid to do the work on yourself and get a sense of calm that it is okay to be yourself. Get emotionally naked. Cry and purge and ask your Higher Power what it is that you bring to the table. Sometimes things are not working in our life because we need to get some things out of our way including ourselves. Recognize your voice of possibility and do not disconnect from your internal wisdom. It is important to be authentic than it is to be accepted. You will achieve more than your identity of who you think you are as long as you think very highly of yourself.

You may feel like you are physically alone but you are never alone. Don't worry about who's not supporting you in the flesh. However, surround yourself with people who get you and you will lead your vision with their support.

Project We Are Free: Women with a Voice is a collection of compelling short stories written by 8 powerful and brave women. These women are using their voice and their stories to help enlighten, encourage, and empower others. The founder of Project We Are Free, Dr. Tamika A. Anderson shares her story of how she transitioned from *"Fear to Freedom"*. Henrietta Hadley shares her experience with how *"Promises"* made in her life shaped and molded her into the phenomenal woman she is today. Kimberly McGowan gives you a glimpse of how she overcame the obstacles in her life and shows you what it will take for you to *"Stand in Your Confidence"*. Virginia Manning shares her courageous story of how she survived teenage and abuse in her chapter entitled, *"The Wish"*. Monique McGilberry shares how every single woman can *"Embrace Your Five-Minute Husband"*. Marchet Fullum shares her story of being a brave toddler who stands up to her mother's abuser in *"No More Wire Hangers"*. KimPossABLE takes us on her journey of rebirth in *"Emergin Spirit"*. Jalila Poole-Lewis awakens us to pay attention to power of three in *"Let Freedom Reign"*. These women are spreading hope as they share the message that you too can overcome challenges and turn your obstacles into opportunities. Follow our journey as we redefine what it means for be FREE.

These women share their stories in a transparent and authentic way to let you know that no matter how hard life's challenges may be, you must have hope that you too will make it through your toughest times.

The women of Project We Are Free have made a non-negotiable decision to be:

Free from living in fear

Free from abuse

Free from financial struggle

Free from the disease to please

Free from suffering

Free from keeping secrets

Free from pretending

Free from playing small

Free from anger

Free from pain

Free from depression

Free from stress

Free from hopelessness

Free from powerlessness

Free from hiding my true self

Free from dimming my light for someone else

Free from not being appreciated

Free from carrying grudges

Free from grief

Free from hurting

Free from settling for less

Free from frustration

Free from irritation

Free from doubt

Free from discouragement

Free from blame

Free from revenge

Free from hatred

Free from pessimism

Free from impatience

Free from rage

Free from insecurity

Free from unworthiness

Free from judgment

Free from procrastination

You too can experience freedom from the things that have kept you tied down from living life on your own terms. We have to also understand that some of the things that are holding us back are lies that we have told ourselves or someone else has told us. It's time to reject these thoughts, actions, and feelings so that we can truly be free.

We want to thank you for taking the time to read this book. But more importantly we want YOU to thank YOU for taking the time out for yourself to read this book. For the women, we are always taking care of others and not taking care of ourselves so we applaud you for reading this book. We are excited to be this journey of healing and freedom with you. We are so proud of you for committing to purging yourself from your past and present shame, suffering, guilt, loss, anger, hurt, resentment, unforgiveness, and the silent pain that you carry on a day to day basis.

It's time to unpack your bag of open wounds and improperly healed scars. I am so glad that you didn't wait until it's too late to take action. Reading this book is a sign that you're ready, ready to execute a different process because you know that the process you are operating in right now is not working. In this book you will laugh, you will cry, and you will gasp but you will have some major shifts and breakthroughs and it will be painful at times but it will require you to let go. Let go of some people, places, and stuff that's been weighing you down mentally, physically, spiritually, emotionally, and financially. It's going to require you to let go of some situationships and toxic relationships that are dragging you down. Let them go so that you can pick up your vulnerabilities. Let yourself see the scared little girl or little boy that is tired of being invisible yet terrified to be seen. We are on this journey to freedom with you so that you know you are not alone.

About
Dr. Tamika A. Anderson

Dr. Tamika A. Anderson is an author, speaker, and Founder of the Project We Are Free. She is also the founder of the Speak Up, Speak Out Movement. Dr. Tamika is a survivor of 20 years of Domestic Violence and Abuse. Inspired by her own Domestic Violence experience, Dr. Tamika's work aims to empower survivors of domestic violence and traumatic experiences through speaking, coaching, and mentoring.

Dr. Tamika's dedication to helping women inspired her to write the #1 International Best-Selling book, **Speak Up & Get Out: A Guide to Survive & Thrive from the Devastation of Domestic Violence**, an urgently needed and insightful guidebook for women to help them know the red flags of domestic violence and how to escape a potentially deadly relationship. Her book can also help supportive family members and friends better understand the dynamics of Domestic Violence.

Dr. Tamika knows from both personal experience and from experience in the trenches with victims and survivors of Domestic Violence that the trauma these women face are both terrifying and universal. Dr. Tamika's goal is to equip women with the tools and strategies they need to overcome their obstacles and live a life free from abuse.

Dr. Tamika holds a Bachelor of Arts in Psychology, a Master of Science in Organizational Leadership, a Doctor of Science in Information Systems & Communications and she is also a Certified Financial Manager through the United States Department of Defense. Dr. Tamika has also been featured on NBC, ABC, HLN, FOX, and Radio One to spread her compelling message of Domestic Violence Awareness.

From Fear to Freedom
Written by: Tamika A. Anderson, D. Sc.

"Let nothing dim the light that shines from within"
~ Maya Angelou

I would love to tell you some made for TV story about my life but I can't. I was just a young girl from the hood with big dreams and an even bigger vision. Back then, if you had told me that my nightmares would turn into dreams and my dream would be my reality and that my nightmares would be long forgotten in some cloud of "I can't believe I survived all of that!". I would have thought for sure you had lost your mind. Here's what I know: My story may not be uncommon, but it was a unique experience that shaped my destiny to find my voice and become free from everything that was holding me back from unpacking my bags of fear and pain. I finally took the time to heal the unhealed wounds that had been bleeding through the scabs of molestation, abuse, loss, and rejection. So many of us have untold stories, unshared experiences that could easily make the difference in the life of another person.

For some of you, your voice has been abused out of you, and silenced. You've unknowingly given someone permission to rob you of your voice. I can't blame you, you didn't know you had the power to protect your voice or even use your voice, and now it's time for you to find it. You need to get used to sharing your voice and finding the value in your voice. You are one voice but your voice matters.

Some of you are being held captive in areas of your life and the door is not even locked. Whether you're locked up in your mind with negative thoughts, a job, a situationship (it's complicated right?), a marriage, depression, anxiety, un-forgiveness, or a relationship that could possibly lead to death, you are falsely imprisoned and you just need help to set yourself free.

We sometimes get into this cycle where things will get good, then get bad, get good then we get hit with what feels like a left upper cut. Your job may be doing you bad, a so called friend has turned their back on you, a family member is spreading untrue rumors about you, and you're an underdog because your relationship at home or because your business is not thriving and you find yourself self-abusing and beating yourself up because you are frustrated with yourself and your life and you keep asking yourself questions like, "How did my life become such a mess?" and "Why am I not where I want to be in life?".

It took me a little time, but I began to awaken to my purpose when I heard these words.

"Mrs. Anderson, do you have any questions?"

"No, I'm just speechless. I just want to start a new life, I just don't know how."

"Mrs. Anderson, you do understand you now have an Access Card to buy food for your daughter."

I remember those words so clearly like it was yesterday. I left that welfare office excited knowing I could now put food on the table. But I also felt a sense of shame & embarrassment that here I was working and going to school yet I had to rely on food stamps as a source of survival to escape abuse. Although I was thankful for being able to have the resourced to buy food, I immediately started thinking, "How am I going to get the food from the grocery store back home without anyone seeing me?". I didn't want anyone to know that I was on welfare. Even though I was afraid to be out this late with my small daughter, I decided to go grocery shopping between 2 and 4 in the morning way across town because I knew the odds of someone knowing me was very slim.

Let's face it, the general public looks down on people who are on welfare. I was so ashamed of having to use my Access Card as a form of payment that I'd swipe the card as quickly as possible hoping not to be seen or heard. My voice had been silenced through abuse as a child and into adulthood and now it was silenced with shame, guilt, embarrassment and feelings of not being good enough because I had to rely on the welfare system for food. I worked hard to finish my degree so that I could break the cycle of being uneducated, abused, and on welfare. I wanted to be free from all of those negative labels. I wanted to help other women who were escaping abuse. I was the poster child for leaving my abuser and going back. My daughter and I had lived out of the car on two different occasions in an attempt to escape the abuse in our home, I quickly learned that the legal system was unfair, and how hard it was hard to start a new life free from abuse.

As a result, I went back to my abuser. Although I wanted to help other women, I realized that my voice had been silenced for too many years. I didn't know I could give myself permission to use my voice. I decided to make a video with notecards about why I finally decided to leave my abuser and even in the video I didn't use my voice, well not my physical voice. That video was retweeted by Queen Latifah to over 6 million people. It was then that I had begun to free myself. I mustered up the courage to speak up and speak out and I'm speaking to you right now- hoping you will find the courage to free yourself from whatever is holding you back.

We must stop judging the value of our message and instead embrace the power and purpose of what we have to say. I share the fears of many who think they do not have a voice: Will they judge me? Will they reject me? I know that there are many people like me who have something to say and are just looking for a conducive environment in which to say it, to cultivate it, and to powerfully present it to the world.

Once I finally got the courage to face some of my deepest truths, a funny but not so funny thing happened after years of abuse and years of being stuck in too many cycles to name. In the 20th year I opened my email to…"Dear Dr. Anderson, attached is the Draft Agreement which I prepared on your behalf. Kindly review it and let me know ASAP if you have any questions or concerns and if you want me to send it to his attorney for his review. I would like to send it to him prior to the final divorce hearing on August 26th."

In that moment, every time I feared for my life and thought I was going to die flashed before my eyes. What had I done? I filed for a restraining order hoping the abuse would stop and instead of no longer abusing me, my abuser filed for a divorce. I didn't want a divorce, I just wanted the abuse to stop. I was devastated. As the day of the final divorce hearing approached I felt a sense of deep sadness. On the day of the final divorce I felt like I was heading to a funeral. It felt like a death. My eyes became blurred as I tried to hold back the tears of coming to the realization that all of our joint hopes, dreams, visions, goals, and future plans were never going to come to pass as a team. No more "I love yous", no more of taking a beating, no more accepting his lies, and no more putting up with his cheating. Today was the day my marriage ended.

As I sat there for hours in the courtroom, my attorney walks up to me and says, "Dr. Anderson you will not be divorced today.". I asked in disbelief, "what do you mean?". She replied, "he and his attorney didn't submit all of their documents and the court is now closed.". I asked, "So what does that mean?" She said, "Well, you'll get a letter in the mail but be sure to show up for the Criminal Domestic Violence hearing next month."

The following month I showed up for the Criminal Domestic Violence hearing because I wanted my voice to heard. I wanted to follow-up on the Civil Protection Order that I had filed. I wanted the judge to hear what had been done to me and our daughter. I wanted to be a voice for the millions of women that had died or were too afraid to speak up and still trapped in the prison of domestic violence and abuse.

When I left the Criminal Court that day when my abuser had been convicted of domestic violence I went straight home.

I fell to the floor into a fetal position in my office and I cried. I cried uncontrollably.

I cried out to God to tell Him that I released my abuser to Him.

I cried out to God asking Him to free me from the situation emotionally, spiritually, and physically.

I cried for the death of my marriage.

I cried for our daughter who had seen and suffered through so much.

I cried because I could no longer show or tell my abuser that I loved him unconditionally.

I cried for the many women that could not do what I'd just done.

I cried tears of joy for finally giving myself permission to have a voice.

My voice wasn't just a form of expression – it was the key to my miracle which is why I believe in unlocking miracles for others. Having the courage to Speak Up & Speak Out doesn't just change your life; but it changes the lives of people who will be inspired by your story like I was as a young woman reading Maya Angelou's "I Know Why the Caged Bird Sings". I know there is some book, some story, that changed your life that way too. If not, it is my hope that this book will change your life. So, why not use your story to change someone else's life?

As I approach the 3rd year anniversary of finding my voice, I know that anything is possible. We are all born into life with struggles; it is the burden of building the endurance to survive and thrive. I never knew I would be on welfare, abused, and have a thriving business birthed out of so much pain, I never thought I would be a widow before the age of 40. But our purpose is to overcome those challenges by learning who we are and believing in ourselves, our destiny, and our legacy depends on it. Today, I want you to find your weapon of choice to conquer your life's challenges. I found mine and it's speaking words of freedom. What I know is to use your voice to change the world, you don't have to be a gifted speaker. You just have to be a person willing to share your story, your life, and your expertise in an uncompromising way.

It's time to tell the next chapter of your life-changing story.

I want you to SPEAK.

Speak up to anyone or anything that goes against your belief system

Position your purpose for profits and help others stand in their power

Excuse no one's abusive and bad behavior towards you in your personal life and in your business

Ask questions, stop suffering in silence if you need help starting or growing your business ASK, if you need to get out of a bad relationship ask for help but whatever you want to achieve in your life you will have to get up off of your…ASK!

Keep going! Do not stop, do not look back, no matter how dark life seems, no matter how bad it gets…keep going, no matter who leaves you, keep going if things don't turn out the way you want them to, just KEEP GOING!

I want to ask you, are you FREE? Are you showing up as the most powerful and profitable version of yourself? Are you living in a proverbial cage like a bird who doesn't know it has the gift of spreading its wings and reaching new heights? Are you letting the things that you don't have, your insecurities, and your obstacles hold you back from showing up powerfully and profitably in your life? I spent over 15 years not showing up as the most powerful and profitable version of myself because I was not free to be me. And when I asked myself the question that I'm asking you today am I showing up as the most powerful & profitable version of myself, the answer was No.

When I looked at the answer and I looked at why I wasn't showing up as powerful and profitable as I could, it was because I was in a dead end situation. I was in an abusive marriage that had no life, I was in a scenario where I was afraid to show up boldly in my own life. I turned down promotions on my job to keep peace in my home, I dimmed my light, neglected long-time friendships, and rejected lucrative business deals all because of the abuse I was experiencing at the hands of my husband. These were just some of the obstacles preventing me from truly being free to live life operating in my purpose.

For those of you not showing up as the most powerful and profitable version of yourself, you will find there is an obstacle in your way. The first thing you have to do is identify the obstacles and then develop strategies on how you're going to remove and overcome the obstacles. You will need to decide how are you going to get beyond this obstacle.

Ask yourself, why is this obstacle holding you back and what are you willing to do about it? I'd like to share with you what I had to do and in that, I hope you find the courage to do what YOU need to do to be free. When I talk about showing up powerfully and profitably I am not talking about how many degrees you have or the length of letters behind your name. I am not talking about how many years you have in your current profession. I am talking about do you have the courage to show up confidently in your life. Too many of us are stuck because of fear. We carrying bags that weigh us down with the:

Fear of losing our freedom

Fear of not being loved

Fear of failure

Fear of success

Fear of not fitting in

Fear of facing your deepest pain

Fear of losing everything

Fear of change

Fear of making a mistake

Fear of being exposed

Fear of not of living lack

Fear of being humiliated

Fear of the unknown

Fear of being judged

Fear of what others will think when you become successful

Fear of your own power

Fear of not being good enough

Fear of being poor

Fear of not getting it right

Fear of being vulnerable

Do you have the courage to step outside of your comfort zone to set yourself free from the fears that are weighing you down? Whether you share your story from the stage, in your private journal or with a therapist you will at the very least experience a sense of peace and freedom.

There is a stigma around going to therapy and many of us are left to suffer in silence trying to process all of our painful emotions alone. As a result, sadness, frustration, grief, shame, guilt, and embarrassment turns into anger.

Don't be ashamed to reach out to someone for help. So much of you has been chipped away. You have wounds that have never been healed and you've been living with them for so long that you've forgotten they are even there. Give yourself permission to be whole again. It's okay to reclaim who you are and regain your freedom. Just because someone has built a prison for you doesn't mean you have to stay in it. Project We Are Free was created to help liberate you from the prisons (financial prison, prison of insecurities, prison of poverty, prison of I'm not good enough) that have you feeling as if you are stuck with no way out. Project We Are Free is a Liberation Movement. The question is, what's holding you back?

To the women especially, we need to have the freedom to choose, freedom from abuse, freedom to be loved, and the freedom to be happy. There are some freedoms that we willingly give up and that's the freedom to live life on our own terms. Some of us also give up the freedom to be financially fit and physically fit because we feed our emotions by blowing our budget with retail therapy and eating food that's no good for our bodies because of the various stressors and traumatic experiences we've had in our lives. We allow too many obstacles to hold us back including negative thoughts of I'm too fat, I'm too old, I'm too ugly, I'm too… and I'm just outright scared.

You're going to need to stop being scared and gain the courage to speak out. The courage to speak out is the thing that can change the world. Some of you have had your voice muted for so long that the businesses that should have been started so long ago, the life you should be living and the dreams you should be fulfilling haven't come to pass because you did not speak out. Oftentimes we like to feel sorry for ourselves and woe is me. But in all of our lives there have been situations where we did not speak up and speak out. When we do choose to speak up and speak out here's the pros of what happens. We have a healthy view of who we are, we have strong boundaries, we prosper, we see life from a positive perspective and from a place of strength and power. When we don't speak out, we are resentful of ourselves and others, we operate from a place of hopelessness, and we feel stuck but we're really not.

We're more than just moms, dads, or someone's daughter or son. We show up in this optically driven world confined to an expression of what's popular today. It's time to get emotionally naked, stop telling these superficial tales of your life, and share your story from a place of authenticity so you can show up as the most powerful and profitable version of yourself.

You'll find that the results you are experiencing in your life are a direct result of the actions you have taken and decisions you've made along your journey. If you find you have one bad thing after another happening in your life than what you define as good things, then you haven't been speaking up and speaking out. If you are experiencing one win after another then congratulations because you have been speaking up and speaking out. Show the world your true value. When you ascend from this earth, you will look back and know that you left a legacy that will change as many lives as there are grains of sand. Infinite possibilities, infinite lives changed, infinite freedom, and infinitely you.

About Henrietta Kay Fountaine -

Daughter of Earl Watson and the late Leona L Fountaine baby sister of Linda Traylor and Proud Mommy of Kayla Hadley. Native of Muskegon, MI, Graduate of Western Michigan University and has lived in PA for over 20 years where she raised her daughter with the love and support of her village who now attends Clark Atlanta University 25 years' experience in Management & Marketing Consulting for both Non- Profit and For-Profit organizations, Post-Secondary Educator, International Speaker and Performer, Conference convener and facilitator Grant Administrator, Domestic Violence Advocate, Workforce and Youth Development expert.

 She is the founder of Star Educational after school youth development programs for girls ages 7 -14 providing life skills, civic engagement, leadership, social and career development in Philadelphia PA. Henrietta has empowered the lives of countless individuals by drawing from her owns personal and professional experiences. She has been recognized by local and national organizations for her commitment and dedication to the women and youth she served across the country.

She has produced a one women play and educational empowerment series called "Promises" depicting and discussing the cycles, affects and signs of Domestic Violence and how it impacts our society.

`Henrietta has been traveling across the country speaking and performing on Domestic Violence to provide awareness and prevention information to assist individuals and families suffering in silence.She is currently in the studio recording a single entitled "Free" dedicated to the life of Sacramental CA school teacher murdered by her husband February 2017.

She is excited about accepting the first group of youth ages 6-18 who will attend summer day & overnight camps design for children who have witnessed Domestic Violence or living without parents murdered due to Domestic Violence.

Promises

Written by: Henrietta Kay Fountaine - Hadley

"Jesus Promised to set you free from every curse of your past"

~ T.D. Jakes

My name Henrietta is the legacy name given to me by my grandmother whom I am named after. I was given the name on the day my mother was scheduled to have an abortion and my Grandmother Promised she would help take care of me and if my mom would allow me to bear her name. My mom was her only daughter. They made this promise sitting in the parking lot of the abortion center and used the money my dad provided for the abortion procedure toward lunch at their favorite restaurant. You will read about promises broken & kept in this chapter. The more I wrote the more I realized my life was built on broken *promises*. God is the Promise Keeper of my life and has restored every broken promise.

My life as daughter, granddaughter, sister, wife, mom, God Mom, Auntie, Cousin, and friend. Not to mention the gifting from my heavenly Father has made room for me to experience greatness with many promises sent by him on this journey of life. God promised "that my latter days would be greater than my former days". I grew up in a small town in Michigan in a community my family founded and developed into a small subdivision of homes and land called Reedsville which also includes our family church and a park with a community center in Muskegon, MI Township.

I lived in this community with my family and friends for 18 years upon graduation from high school and moved to Kalamazoo, MI to attend college after I graduated from college right on schedule. I started my professional career in the world of corporate Management, Post-secondary education teaching classes in management & merchandising departments at various colleges. I am also a Leader in public policy advocating for women and girls discussing issues concerning domestic violence.

My life has been mentored by women who have shared their lives and gifts with me to become the woman of courage I am today. My contribution to Project We Are Free 2017 is to help men and women look into their hearts for brokenness that happened during childhood and see what needs mending as an adult. I want to encourage and share hope that forgiveness is the key and love makes you whole again. Promises has been written to empower others to free themselves from secrets and seek help to live a healthy life full of potential and prosperity.

Writing this chapter for "Project We Are Free" has been liberating by providing another level of healing and forgiveness. I want others to empower themselves with the resources to love themselves first in order to trust and love others. I decided to dedicate this chapter to my mommy my biggest fan Leona L. Fountaine, known by our family members as Lee and referred to by her students as Ms. Fountaine. I will be forever grateful for the promise made between her and my Grandmother that spared my life to help others live the life they were born to live through my gifts of encouragement.

My mom found her truth and won the many battles of life before leaving earth!

She kept her Promise to herself to live her Best life in her latter years. I made peace with her and I was Blessed to hear her tell me over and over again how PROUD she was of me and the mother I had become for my daughter. I have no doubt in my mind about whether or not I kept my Promise made to her as a little girl that I would make her proud of me when I became a grown woman. Although it seemed like I went through hell sometimes to keep it.

She confirmed that my Promise to her had been kept when she phoned me very early one morning which I am sad to say would also be our last conversation before she died on February 12, 2006 she went on and on to tell me how much she loved me and encouraged me to keep God first and never give up the fight of life. The opportunity to share these life experiences to encourage others to stay on life's journey and unpack the emotional baggage along the way and don't let fear rob you of your dreams that are intended to provide a life of hope and happiness!!!

This chapter is a springboard to upcoming Promises Empowerment journals and self- care workbooks that have been written to help hurting hearts heal. Visit my web site www.PromisePrograms.com & Facebook Page for more information.

Follow me on the path of *promises*, broken branches built on rich soil in my life.

My parents made a childhood pinky *promise* at the ages of 10 and 12 to remain best friends for life, get married, and raise a family. My mom became a teen mother at 17 and my dad was sent to the military at 18 and their childhood *promise* of marriage was BROKEN! The secrecy of raising a child together out of wedlock while remaining best friends and married to other spouses with families in different cities in the state of Michigan. This *promise* was kept until my mother's sudden death in 2006. To this very day my dad is always ready to share a fond child hood memory of the sixty-year friendship he and my mom shared together. My dad kept his *promise* to raise me and make sure I was a part of his life and knew my eight siblings from his twenty-year marriage. My life's foundation was built on love and support.

At age seven, I knew I would be singing and entertaining for a living, a lifestyle I always *promised* myself and family. These dreams were always in my sight and on my lips. Family and friends believed in my dreams and by age nine I was being groomed for greatness and nothing I mean NOTHING could stop me from keeping the *promises* I made to myself and family. Little did I know there would be a derailment at age 10 on my life journey filled with *promise*. I was molested by a step - father who also beat my mom if she worked too much overtime on her job as registered nurse. PROMISES took on a different role in my life at age ten. I must promise not to tell my mom or family that I was being forced to touch my stepfather's penis while he fondled me every Saturday while my mom was working. My sister was away at college, my grandmother at choir rehearsal, and my grandfather a Police Officer across the street asleep. My step-father threatened to kill my whole family that I loved dearly. I kept that *promise*. I know it was WRONG! My mom kept a *promise* to herself and ended her abusive marriage, which ended my childhood sexual abuse and we were back on the *promise* path of our life. I kept my secrets of pain and embarrassment of sexual abuse packed in my personal baggage instead of sharing with my mom during her divorce process. I got really good at hiding my childhood secret with over achieving in my performing arts and extra-curricular activities.

While she was determined she would take her life back, she gave me everything she thought I needed to be a strong girl after surviving her own domestic violence. She enrolled me in Girl Scouts, charm classes, and any program that would build my self-esteem to teach me how to survive in a world where the only thing you could rely on is your faith in God. She made me PROMISE to read the entire Bible Verse Psalm 27 whenever I needed encouragement. She kept her *Promises* to provide for me as a single parent working as a nurse and she kept that *promise* until she died. She never remarried.

I was able to unpack the baggage I carried for 23 years about my childhood abuse.

I broke the *promise* I made as a child to my abuser. I shared with my mom before I gave birth to my only child in 1996. I was free from bondage that derailed my life as child. It's hard to believe I hid this baggage during my middle school years as a bully, my high school days as an over- achiever, and my college years suffered from the need to please everyone disease while suffering in silence. Before my college graduation I suffered in silence through two campus date rapes by two different prominent fraternity brothers who were upper classmen. It was another derailment on the *Promise* journey. I kept PRESSING! Now I ask myself if I was really hiding or was my baggage of sexual abuse being exposed through my behaviors and patterns as a young adult. I added more pounds to the hidden baggage I would carry in my broken heart for the next 14 years without exposing my sexual assaults on my path of *Promise*. I was hiding this baggage fairly well and moving along with life while accomplishing my planned career goals as a professional black woman in male dominated management position in Corporate America. My journey was running smoothly as a workaholic with an eating disorder and looking for love in all the wrong men. My hidden baggage was starting to burst at the seams and zippers. I still managed to keep *promises* I made to my family and friends at seven years old to make them proud. All the while I am breaking inside with hurt and pain from all the broken *promises* not kept by others in my adult life as a 21-year-old woman. A Lot has happened since I *promised* myself at seven years old that I would be a famous vocalist around the world!

Proverbs 18:21

"The tongue has the power of Life & Death"

Life as an adult was really taking off and everything I touched was tuning to gold. My career was soaring. I was teaching in post-secondary education in my field of study, singing with a jazz band and performing musical theater, but I was reminded daily of my unwanted baggage. It showed up in my poor decision making. Through my personal disappointments, I decided to move away from Michigan and start a new life in California and pursue my music career full-time and entertain around the world. I jumped back on the path of my life *Promises* without realizing the baggage full of secrets would travel with me no matter where I moved as long as it was buried in my broken heart. I had no idea how to begin my healing and forgiveness until one day I was watching OPRAH. She revealed she had been sexually abused. I realized at 25 years old, I wasn't the only black professional woman who had been sexually abused as a child. I thank God for Oprah and her transparency! Her truth set me free.

My prayer is for this chapter of my life is to set someone free from their bondage, like Oprah did for me. I used the key of forgiveness to heal my broken heart to live a healthy life without unresolved hurt and pain from past experiences, who may be too embarrassed to share with anyone until it may be too late.

My move to California was taking off in the right direction. Auditions were scheduled, demos shopped, and studio time arranged. I was on my way to taking my rightful place center stage. I received a call about an original demo I sent to Jimmy Jam & Terry Lewis, yes the same music producers that produced Janet Jackson's Control Album. They were impressed with my cover demo and asked me to send three original songs with a two-week deadline.

I was working in San Diego, California at Fashion Institute of Design and Merchandising (FIDM) campus working with Design & Merchandising students making a name for myself. I had been recently nominated for outstanding faculty of the year by the graduating class and selected to sing for the sold out annual Golden Hanger Fashion Award Dinner in downtown San Diego. There were tons of studio work in Los Angeles (LA) and plenty of people to meet and I was willing to do whatever it took to reach my dreams and keep my *promise* to myself to one day be a star in the music industry. I was taking the red – eye flights back and forth to LA from San Diego daily to meet studio schedules and meetings with A& R directors in the music industry to discuss opportunities for my career. I was doing what it took to make it in California.

"You know you're on the right path when your dreams start believing in you"

~ Tyler Perry

I watched Tyler Perry share his story on The T.D Jakes Talk Show October 25, 2016. He shared the above quote concerning his life after being homeless with a few dollars in his pockets and overcoming his childhood abuse in the 1990s. Now Tyler Perry's worth $600 million in 2017 and living a life of fame and fortune after all the *Promise* derailments in his life. It made me reflect back to 1992 on my days of *PROMISE* in California before marriage and motherhood took over my life.

I will never forget that day on Friday, September 15,1992. My girlfriend invited me for lunch in beautiful La Jolla Cove at Nordstrom café to catch up on everything happening in my life since my move to California. We were sitting there enjoying our meal and he walked by.

It was like the angels had just released him from heaven! Tall, skin the color of gold, and charm that would capture every fish in the sea. He was Just FINE and I wanted to know who he was. I waited a while to see if there was a woman or any children on his team. I made my way to the counter where he was placing his order and did the old- school approach by asking him if he attended college nearby. He went on to say he was not from the area. He said he was from Michigan, "are you kidding me. I replied, "so am I!". We smiled and started a long conversation that led to exchanging phone numbers. I was on top of cloud nine doing cartwheels. Fast forward to the next three months and we were dating and spending all our time together. I found my Prince Charming and my fairytale had now begun. Our love and compassion for one another was overwhelming. We were inseparable. He was everything I dreamed about, I just can't remember this ever being a part of my dream. Meeting my Prince Charming and living a fairytale was never a part of my *promise* path and I was being setup for another derailment I did not see coming.

I was blindsided by the charm that lifted the load of my baggage filled with pain and secrets I brought with me from Michigan and still dragging along on my *PROMISE* journey in California.

Put on your seat belt and prepare for a roller-coaster ride of love with Beauty and the Beast in 3- D. Grab your glasses while you have a chance. In over three months of dating my Prince was unbelievable and spoiling me had no limits. Love was all over us. We were finishing each other's sentences. I couldn't live without him. I made a *PROMISE* to him I would never let us go and no one would ever come between us. I even shared a little about my family and childhood, all the good things, of course. He was the father of two with different moms, had been divorced and two engagements that ended before they made it to the altar. Red Flag, my thoughts were their loss, my gain. I would lose focus on my music and goals and the Promises that had brought me to Cali, not to mention I missed my deadline with famous music producers, appointments with music agents, and A&R directors. You name it, I was missing out on opportunities left and right.

We were soaking in a beautiful hot tub after the most delish dinner made by my Prince soon to be my King when he asked if he could attend my fast approaching music showcase in Long Beach, CA where I would be performing with local and well known rappers popular in the Hip Hop industry today with reality shows to match. I was set to perform for major record label executives shopping for new acts to sign. He insisted we drive his car instead of catching the Red Eye flight to the showcase (Red Flag) I informed him that traffic was always a bear and hard to navigate and we should fly. He assured me he knew what he was doing. I missed my first performance and arrived late. The rap artists and managers that hired me were pissed and had no problem with letting me know how I showed disrespect to the music opportunity and broke THE code of ethics by being late but, (Red Flags) My Prince jumped in my manager's face with a few choice words and announced to me and everyone else he was my new manager and he would be handling all my business as far as my music career. Really? He knew nothing about business, not to mention the music business. My friends kept asking me the same question over and over again "Where did this guy come from?".

Over the next few weeks I was scheduled to move from downtown San Diego to LA to be closer to the music industry and start working on my original music project. Of COURSE that never had a chance of happening. I was blinded by love and everything My Prince Charming had to offer and I mean EVERYTHING!!!

I never thought my Prince Charming of my DREAMS would become the Monster in my Nightmares!!!!!!!

Keep reading & Pay close attention to the Red Flags along my path of Promise.

My move to LA never happened, instead I moved to Chula Vista, CA with my Prince Charming a far cry from downtown San Diego where I walked to Sea Port Marina daily for exercise and fantasize over the fancy boats and where I would dock my boat when I landed my first record deal. LOVE will make you do some crazy things when you're filling the voids of hurt and pain. I knew I couldn't "SHACK UP" with him, a word my family used when you live with your boyfriend before you were married (common practice today). *I promised* my family I would not shame their name and I explained this family value to him and (Red flag) a week later he asked me for my hand in marriage. Keep in mind he's the father of two children, divorced and two failed engagements and estranged from his family. (Red Flag) While deciding whether to have a big or small wedding he was offered a promotion on his job that would relocate him to the east coast in 30 days and he ask me to move with him on East Coast with the plans that I would commute to LA from Pennsylvania (PA) weekly to pursue my music. Now I look back and say to myself, "Really, do you think this would happen? Let's not forget I have the need to please disease, I'm just saying"!

Fast forward to a Small Chapel on our Wedding day just my Prince & I getting married with only two witnesses the minister and his wife. Friends and family were not invited I had been convinced this was our sacred time (Red Flag) and my close friend had witnessed verbal abuse while visiting one day and was honest enough to tell me that she could not witness or agree to my marriage to him due to the way he treated me in her presence. Red Flags flying high and I was blinded by love!!!

OVER the next four years, we would have trouble in our marriage with manipulation on both our parts, playing the hide & seek game with past secrets of pain and sorrow as children, young adults, and full-grown adults with responsibility to others and ourselves.

He hid his demons of hurt and abandonment and I hid my baggage of pain and embarrassment, which got in the way to love & happiness.

Our marriage was spinning out of control and no matter how much I poured into my husband and reassured him I would never leave like all the others he didn't believe me. I later found out why everyone had used the exit door out of his life.

I discovered my Prince was living a life of deception and BROKE his promise to me with multiple marital affairs and a pornography addiction. I confronted him with my proof and evidence and keep in mind this was during the no cell phone era. You know how our investigative skills kick in when it comes to our MAN.

All I remember to date is being thrown against the wall and forcefully strangled and he told me never to question him again. I broke away with disbelief and *promised* myself never to make him that angry that he would put his hand on me. I *promised* myself if he ever put his hand on me again I would leave. He also Promised he would never put his hands on me again and made me Promise I would not push his buttons to make him that angry. (Red Flag) He bought me a dog the next day to keep me company because he would work extra hours and shower me with a lavish lifestyle while hiding his demons and me holding on to my marriage for the sake of not wanting to disappoint my family with a failed marriage that would end in divorce after four years.

Our Roller-coaster of love would continue and I knew we needed to get help or one of us would not make it out of this marriage alive. We had been trying to start a family and after the last attempt to strangle me (Red Flag) I often wonder if he was trying to damage my throat where GOD placed one of my many gifts? just a thought. NEVER REALLY THOUGHT ABOUT IT UNTIL I STARTED WRITING THIS CHAPTER for the book project.

I scheduled a Dr.'s appointment to get back on birth control and was planning my return back to Cali. To my surprise my Dr. informed me after taking a routine pregnancy test that I should call my husband because we were EXPECTING a child and I was in my first trimester. Are you kidding me??

Me being me I hope to save my marriage I took our pregnancy as a *promise* sign from God to save and restore our marriage with this gift of our child. We decided to come clean with each other with our secrets of abuse and abandonment issues. We asked God for forgiveness. for our mistakes. I decided to break free from my bondage of hurt & embarrassment from sexual molestation and tell my mom. I hoped to press charges against my step father. He was dead and The Statue of Limitations was on his side due to the time frame. It felt good to unpack that baggage and burn it. I no longer wanted to carry that baggage while I carried my child. He started communicating with his family and he and his mother dealt with his abandonment issues with his father and the relationship he never had chance to foster due to his mother leaving his father when he was a small child and he never forgive her for that and really hated her during adult hood which led to his hatred toward women.

We decided to get help and attend counselling and deal with our issues from our childhood that were preventing us from sharing our life together in love with oneness to God.

My husband and his abandonment issues from being taken from his dad, to never meet again and me with my sexual abuse and date rape issues that would prevent me from trusting men.

We were on our way to healing from our past and starting a new life with healed hearts of forgiveness for those who hurt us and for one another.

My new music anthem for our marriage became the "Battle is not yours it's the Lord's"

We started living our lives according to word of God and I believed God would provide my husband the knowledge to lead our family. We joined a local church and begin to work in ministry together. I had been brought up as a child in church all my life and was pleased we could provide a spiritual foundation for our child. God began to use us in a mighty way. My husband would later be installed as the youth pastor of our church and God was taking my music ministry to another level and GOD

WAS USING OUR TRIALS AND TEST TO HELP OTHER COUPLES WITH THEIR FAILING MARRIAGES! We were able to rejoice over how God saved our marriage to help new couples with their marriage according to God's word and we started a marriage ministry in our home. I began to learn about Domestic violence in order to help other women suffering in silence. I attended trainings and workshops with the plans to start a community awareness group for men and women suffering from abuse.

Over the next seven years we would raise our daughter together she was the apple of our eye and we were really moving and shaking in our local community. I had been asked to sing on Bobby Jones BET Gospel music show. We decided I would go back to work full time and work with women returning to workforce. I started learning women issues and healing from abuse and became an advocate and was asked to speak to a group of women ABOUT Abuse at Muncy State Prison the only Female prison in the state of PA.

I decided to create a one woman Play called PROMISES depicting the cycles of LOVE & the stages OF abusive RELATIONSHIPS with violence. I met women with stories that would reduce me to tears and was given a poster about the life of Cyd Berger a severely battered women who had been incarcerated since 1980 doing life without parole. I will share more about her in Promises Workbook. After the debut of Promises the one-woman show infused with music, poetry and dance, I began to travel all over the Commonwealth of Pennsylvania to perform Promises with panel discussions and become an DV advocate with resources to help those suffering in silence. Promises was being recognized with awards on a local & state level for the services I was providing to bring awareness to stop and prevent Domestic Violence. I became the EMPOWERMENT Expert and was creating a community of empowered men & women. I became compassionate for others suffering with the same problems I overcame and wanted to see them whole in their life to live the life GOD HAD INTENDED FOR THEM before they were robbed of their freedom.

I was preparing my acceptance speech for the "Women of the year award" given to an individual with leadership and dedication toward a mission Domestic Violence and child sexual abuse was my main focus to find a way to STOP & PREVENT!! Remember the two childhood love birds my mom and dad. They would travel to Pennsylvania to attend the award dinner with me where I would receive the WOMEN of the Year from a national organization for my commitment and dedication to women & girls issues. The picture perfect family (Red Flags) would have made all to see proud of our image. I should have known things were going too well.

A week after the award dinner my world turned upside down! I was lying in the middle of the street, cars coming from both directions, my husband was over me and my seven-year-old daughter was crying "I want my MOMMY!".

About
Kimberly McGowan

Kimberly lives in Milwaukee, WI with her husband of 18 years and their two children. She has a master's degree in education and plans to earn her doctoral degree as well, feeding her strong hunger to learn more about human behavior. As CEO and founder of Professional Singles. My core belief is that God did not intend for man to be alone and everyone has a soul mate - even those who think they are too busy to find love. There is someone, somewhere, waiting for you!

Kimberly understands the importance of giving back. She is a philanthropist who volunteers her time helping with programs that empower women and young adults. Kimberly's credentials also include: International Association of Professional Life Coaches and International Membership of Professional Advisors, Coaches & Trainers.

Stand in Your Confidence
Written by: Kimberly McGowan

"When you're different, sometimes you don't see the millions of people who accept you for what you are. All you notice is the person who doesn't."

~ Jodi Picoult, Change of Heart

Do you know who you are, who you were destined to become? I didn't either but I discovered myself through the trial and tribulations of life. Who we are is not defined by our family, friends, co-workers, children, or spouse. No, it's not any of those things who are in defined by the thoughts, opinion or judgement of others. We are all created to do something different than anyone else on this planet and that makes everyone of fascinating, unique human being. Not one of us is the same; why do people want others to behave the way they would behave or say what they would say. Knowing who you are is standing firm in your truth and believing in the power of YOU. It is the bravest gift you can give yourself. How easy is it to blend in and become camouflaged with the crowd? Bloom like the flower you are and spread your scent of love and talent all over the universe. There is no other like you on the planet; because there is only one of you there are no blueprints and whatever mishaps you make in life you were supposed to make those mistakes for growth, knowledge, and power. Knowing that there no mistakes in life what are your dreams, goals, and hopes for the future? There is no such thing as a goal that's too big to accomplish. If it came to you it can move through you. Never be ashamed of who you are or the past that you come from. Confront the past deal and move past them because your past does not belong in your present.

The experiences of yester years have taught me what I will and will not accept, who to let into my personal space and who to avoid. It's important to be selective with the company that you keep and the people you share information with. Is this person giving your life or is this person slowly taking your breath away. Part of standing in your confidence means knowing your worth. It is never wise to let others speak negatively about you in your presence, but growing up I needed someone to standup for me when I couldn't stand up for myself. I would absorb and accept every negative comment like a sponge; those comments left a permanent scar on the heart. After a while like anything else the scar starts to grow a scab and the wound eventually heals but the scar of that pain never goes away. Do not allow anyone to disrespect you at all period. Not allowing other people to disrespect means you must respect yourself. This is something else that I had to learn because I was not taught this virtue.

What I realized is that comes after loving yourself. These experiences from early childhood through young adult have made me who I am today. I am confident to the point where some may think I'm arrogant but that could not be further from the truth. I walk and talk with confidence because this is who I am known and every day I must remind that girl in the mirror that I am a woman of purpose. So don't judge my stride unless you know my story. I can recall growing up and not having the best clothes or the latest hair style. I got made fun of I was called nappy headed, big nose, and fat, it was so bad that when I got a Jeri curl I was told I needed to write the people that made the Jeri curl because my regular hair was so too nappy. I remember being told that my nose covered half my face it was so wide. The worst was finding out that people thought I was going to be a loser because they felt my parents were losers and therefore you are bound to be the same. See some would say that I was supposed to be a single mother, living on the system with no hope, and no future and basically a whore. As if those comments weren't bad enough I was told that "You will never find someone that will marry you" ah that shattered my world. The worse part about these memories is that it came from family. The ones that are supposed to care and love you the most are the ones that can do the most irreversible damage. The place where I should feel the safest is the place where I hurt the most. I had to release the shame and guilt that I felt for being me. It is OK to have dark chocolate skin, to have thick hips, and full juicy lips, and a slightly wide nose? Yes, it is, and I would not change one thing about the shell that I was given. The confidence of being honest, having integrity, purpose, and the desire to help others and make a contribution to the world is what matters!

How do we stand in confidence, by standing in our truth? It takes courage to stand even if you are standing by yourself. Self-confidence is a must in order to succeed in life. If you don't believe in yourself no one else will. No one can advocate for you better than you. You have to be your number one fan and cheerleader. When we are our true selves others will become offended for no reason. They will think you are doing the most and that is ok, we must be ok with that. Be proud of who you are and what you believe in, lean on your integrity. That gut feeling is your intuition speaking to you and guiding you to your truth.

I use to be concerned about the opinion of others because I wanted to be liked and accepted, in order to blend in with others. I was never designed to fit in I was created by the all mighty to stand out. Although no one wants to be an outcast because of the shame and loneliness that sometimes comes along with it can be unbearable. When you understand the bigger picture and bigger purpose, for your life you will start to live a burden free life. I always felt that I would have a decent life, but the life I've created has been more that I hoped for had I listened to the negativity that was spit at me I would not be here today, but I refused to give those words life. I learned to fight and not with my hands but with my mind. I knew that if I got an education I could build a different world and that I could have whatsoever I say and whatsoever I want to create. I've always believed in my inner strength, today I know that voice as the Holy Spirit. Marriage has taught me about trust, friendship, respect, and a new dimension of self-love.

Throughout my marriage I had a fear of being betrayed. I had the hardest time of letting go and trusting another person because of what was told to me. I subconsciously carried the negative stigma from the past into my marriage without realizing it. I questioned if he truly loved me, could he truly me, and am I truly worthy of love. It pains to me to know that I purposefully wanted my husband to leave me because of what others had to say about my worth. I have this amazing man, not perfect, but amazing husband.

One day I had an epiphany and realized that I was creating problems where there were no problems. It was as if God removed the blinders and I was able to see that I had the marriage I dreamt about. From there everything around me changed because I understood that I am not what they said I was. The circles of relationships I choose are those that want the best for me; those relationships that inspire and encourage, but also will speak truth without judgement. I owe no one an explanation of my life choices and I understood that I had to stop trying to be a people pleaser. Allowing my actions to speak is the best way to respond. I am not perfect and that is a good thing. I have a long way to go I am just getting started. When people start to say the opposite of what you and GOD have to say walk away. I understood that being vulnerable to the person that loves and wants to grow with is ok. Hurt people hurt people and I was done causing hurt. It was time for healing.

The lack of confidence that I carried led me to have anxiety and depression. Trying to be what others wanted me to be was slowly killing me. I found myself in the ER on numerous occasion thinking was having a heart attack; nope I was having panic attacks. Performance anxiety was kicking my butt. I had to perform for my employer, I had to perform for associates, and I had to perform for family. Every decision I made was for other people that didn't matter. I had allowed myself to think that I needed to be perfect, which is total nonsense. The beautiful thing about failure is that it teaches us what not to do. The most successful people in life have failed, so there is nothing wrong with not being perfect.

Now that I am able to stand in my own truth and be who I was created to be I am much happier. I am set free from bondage and the shackles of others. My truth is that I desire all the things that God has for me, love, happiness, success, wealth, health. At this point in life I have a clear understanding on how to drown out the background noise. Knowing that I am good enough and worthy enough helps to keep me standing strong. Not to mention the daily practice of meditation and prayer. No longer do I repeat the negative things of the past. For those that desire to be free I encourage you break free from all negativity and start to see yourself in light in which you were created. See the beauty and uniqueness within. When you are confident in you and what you are doing there is no need to tell the world. The actions displayed will speak volumes for you.

I found my confidence by accepting the things I can never

change and focusing on the things that make me great and unique! Who hasn't felt like they've made mistakes? I know now those were mistakes just my patch being redirected. Today is about loving me for who I am and who I am becoming. Someone once said that "there will always be someone prettier, smarter, and younger, but they will never be you! To all my Kings and Queens pick up your crowns place it on your head and start moving. We got work to do!

"Because one believes in oneself, one doesn't try to convince others. Because one is content with oneself, one doesn't need others' approval. Because one accepts oneself, the whole world accepts him or her."

~ Lao Tzu

About Virginia Manning

Virginia Manning is a licensed Professional Counselor and licensed chemical dependency counselor with 13 years of experience in education and counseling. She is currently a high school counselor and has a private practice in Houston, Texas.

Her passion is to motivate, inspire, guide and support others to overcome life's common challenges related to mental health and addiction. She is the CEO of GinMan Consulting and the founder of the Push Pass Life Movement and Destined to Rise: Circle of Success programs. She is the author of *Master Your Journey: Simple Ways to Push Pass Life* and *365 Pushes: Motivation to Overcome Any Challenge.*

Through her dedication to her Mother, Minnie Lee, her passion is to wipe out stigma that hinders life- long success. She lives each day of her life purpose driven and dedicated to helping you live your best life ever.

The Wish

Written by: Virginia Manning, LPC-S, LCDC

Pain nourishes courage. You can't be brave if you've only had wonderful things happen to you.

~ Mary Tyler Moore

Summer 1985, there were fourteen months before my freshman year at Central High School. I had been shy and nerdish all my life and was ready for a change. One day, star dazed and looking up into the night's sky, I made my wish.

Before the Wish….

My first sight of him, he was zooming by our house on a rusty go-cart. His speed caught my attention. My sister, mother and I had been living on Arabella in Beaumont, Texas for about one year. His family was new to the neighborhood and lived right around the corner. That same day, I realized I could look right out of my sister's bedroom window and see clear across the backyard to their back porch.

Later that week, all the neighborhood kids were waiting in line for a ride on the speed machine. My turn was our first close encounter and neither one of us could stop smiling. I got on the back of the seat behind him. I held on for the ride of my life while he dangerously turned the corner and made the block. I could tell that he really liked me.

Our families instantly bonded. My older sister started dating his older brother. And his quest to win me over as his girlfriend began.

After the wish….

Two summers later under the moonlight, he asked me once again to be his girlfriend. The conversation this time was not like his other pleas for my return of affection. He was tired of being turned down. The next sentence after the infamous question was, "This is my last time asking you to be my girlfriend." Instantly, the recollection of the wish flashed into my mind.

I could hear my heart pounding in my chest. Unbeknownst to my immaturity, my answer determined the fate of my next eight years. I hesitated and waited for my heart to slow down before responding. I was seconds away from saying "no" for probably the 100th time. I looked up into the star- studded night, saw the twinkle of the brightest star and mumbled "yes".

The smile on his face after I accepted his hand to be his was one of the few times I can remember him looking at me as if he hit the $1,000,000 jackpot. No one saw or felt the turnaround of that Kool- aid smile like I did. We both were in high school and soon we started skipping school together. We would sneak off campus, catch the city bus to his brother's apartment or wherever we could hide during the school day. My grades dropped from A's and B's to C's and D's. I ended up in afterschool detention a couple of times for skipping classes. I transformed from a good girl to a girl gone. I still maintained good enough grades to remain in school, but he soon dropped out.

Next stop, teenage pregnancy....

My mother totally trusted me. She never suspected that her 14 year old daughter and 17 year old boyfriend were having sex. She trusted me so much that she would often let him spend the night and even sleep in the same bed.

The innocent stunts came to an end when my sister caught us on the front room floor naked. And she broke her neck running down the street to my Mom's friend house to snitch me out. The next month, I missed my period. Nine months later, I experienced the most painful tummy ache imaginable. The cure was the birth of a beautiful baby girl at the age of 16. The $1,000,000 smile on his face had resurfaced.

And the abuse begins....

So now there is a baby involved. In his convoluted world that meant he was officially my property owner. He wanted full control over his estate. When he felt like that control was threatened, he aggressively made his point known of having it returned.

Even though I had a baby now, I still had to finish school because Minnie Lee was not having it. Every morning at 6:45 AM he would meet me and walk me to the school bus stop four blocks away. There were many mornings that I never got on the bus.

I remember one morning of missing the bus so vividly. It was the first time I met the wrath of his hands. I felt like I was in a boxing match, and I was the defeated opponent.

That morning he made sure I missed the school bus again because he thought my pants were too tight (they were absolutely not), and I had on too much make-up (I only had on eyeliner). He pushed me around during the four block walk back home. We went into the tin garage to finish the unwarranted matchup.

Inside the garage, the noise of my head banging against the tin lining was loud and thunderous. I wished my mother who was a few yards away inside the house would hear my gasps of defeat. I wanted and needed to be rescued.

One day I thought I was saved. During a banging session, the back door of the house opened, the pounding inside the tin garage abruptly stopped. Silence…. The back door closed. The banging resumed. The tin lined garage became our frequently reoccurring morning boxing ring.

Countless times, his stress relief sessions seemed like hours. He would eventually calm down and apologize. I would smile as if everything is okay. Once excused from the session, I would turn around and numbingly walk into the house. I would blurt another excuse of why I missed the bus to my mom and drag to my bedroom with my head down. I tearfully closed my eyes, and exhaustedly fell asleep. A few hours later, he was knocking at the back door with a pack of diapers for the baby.

It's 1990. I'm 18 and have my high school diploma. Now it's time to move from under momma's roof and into an apartment with my property owner. I was on my way to a state of totally enslaved freedom. In nine months, he will reconfirm the property contract with a junior, our second child.

My property owner did work Monday through Friday, 8AM- 5PM to provide for his family. After work, his (mind) shift changed. He had to make it home to perform his check on my daily activities.

Of course, his mind told him his ability to tele-control my daily activities were unsatisfactory. Next his mind told him to show me who is in control. Finally, his mind concluded "torture".

Every day he had a property inventory list to check for quality control. Every day my thoughts were on passing the inspection with satisfactory scores. Every day his checklist was riddled with red marks. Every day I failed. Every wrong answer had a consequence.

Question #1 on the inventory checklist:

Did you sit on the porch today?

My 1st time response: Yes, I let the kids play outside for a little while. (Wrong Answer)

Note to self: Learn from your mistakes.

My next time answer to question #1 on the inventory checklist: No, I didn't. The remote controller's response: "Looks like you been sitting outside while I was at work." (There is no correct answer to an abuser's question)

Question #2 on the inventory checklist:

What did you do today?

My 1st time response: I was reading a book. I still plan to go to college. (Wrong Answer)

The remote controller's response: Tear up and hide all books and magazines.

Note to self: Everybody who is with you is not for you.

My next time answer to question #2 on the inventory checklist: Nothing, watching t.v. and cooking. (Education is the key to freedom)

Question #3 on the inventory checklist:

Where did you get those new clothes from?

My 1st time response: I went shopping with my sister today. (Wrong Answer)

Note to self: Those who are in pain and feel bad about themselves want you to feel and look bad also.

My next time answer to question #3 on the inventory checklist: The clothes are for my sister. I borrowed them. She is coming to get them tomorrow. (Outsmart your opponent)

The remote controller's response: "Don't do that shit again."

In his mission to control my life, he eventually lost control of his life. Within a year, he had developed an uncontrollably bad addiction to crack cocaine. He was home less frequently, but the abuse did not decrease.

I started to pray every day.

I prayed for strength. I prayed for guidance. I prayed for a way out.

I got strength. I got guidance. I got a way out.

Then there was a new inventory checklist. It was designed through answered prayers. The new inventory checklist had control over me. There were no wrong answers.

The new question #1 on the new inventory checklist:

How did you get away?

My only answer to the new question #1 on the new inventory checklist: I used spiritual strength and guidance to escape. (Correct Answer)

Note to self: Prayers are more effective than wishes.

My additional answer to the new question #1: Life is about learning lessons from the mistakes you make.

After the prayers….

I developed the strength and guidance to take actions and get away from my property owner. One morning after I gave him the wrong answer, he left to satisfy his drug craving. With evidence on my body of giving the wrong answer and baby #3 forming in my belly, I quickly dressed my kids and myself. All four of us caught the city bus and headed to the police station to press charges for domestic violence. I had finally been courageous enough to stand up for myself. A few weeks later, he was arrested and served almost a year in jail. By Fall, I was registered for the prerequisite classes for the nursing program at Lamar University. I never looked back. I never made a wish again.

About
Monique McGilberry

Monique McGilberry is a poet, and author of the devotional book of poetry, "Your Savior". She is hopefully optimistic about her future and that of women everywhere who are in the healing process. You can follow her on Facebook, Pinterest, and Instagram.

email: MissMonique285@gmail.com

Instagram: MissMonique285

Facebook and Pinterest: Monique McGilberry

Embrace Your Five-Minute Husband
Written by: Monique McGilberry

The search for love and acceptance can lead you to some painful places. This is the conclusion I came to upon many days, months, and years of self-reflection.

In everything that happens to me, good, bad, or indifferent, I'm always searching for the reason and the lesson behind it.

As a woman who identifies more with being labeled as one who has learned how to thrive, when writing this excerpt, I was careful not to focus too heavily on rape, physical, and verbal abuse. Shining light on abuse gives the abuser and the incident power. I'm convinced the power lies in the ability to stand and tell someone else about a chapter in the book of my life that didn't kill me. In fact, it made me want to live all the more.

When you are searching for acceptance and love before you love and accept yourself, some ugly situations can occur. You will see love- because that's what you want to see- where there is none. And you will accept the unacceptable and supply the excuses for it. You will not treat yourself or others with care and loving kindness because you're seeking and "loving" out of fear.

This realization allowed me to forgive others and forgive myself. It also gave me the ability to see myself in the ugly situations. It didn't happen overnight. For years, I played the victim. For years, I acted out in my own anger. And for years I didn't love myself, so I attracted the energy I put out.

Loving yourself is a journey and a daily exercise. You have to be strong enough to see past your errors, past your mistakes, past what happened, and forward to the person you desire to become, flaws and all. Laughing helps. Treating yourself helps. Making your own choices and owning your own power helps.

Abuse is not a gender related issue. It is about power and control. Women who have been abused need kind, strong men in their lives. We need men, not to complete or heal us, but to encircle us with the covering masculine essence only they can provide. Also, we need men to stand with us and expose abuse where they see it.

Men: teach your sons to respect women. Teach them about how positively they impact your own life. If you need help yourself, please get it. Not just for you, but for future generations that come from you.

When we come together and have authentic dialogue, reason with one another, and decide to truly love, the enemy loses, and one more child has parents who demonstrate love in action. One more child sleeps well at night knowing they are safe, and that child goes on to build relationships, God willing, in real love.

I am a survivor for all intents and purposes. Despite the things that have happened, I refuse to live my life as a victim. Perhaps, I could, if I chose to, but that would be taking the easy and simple way out.

When I was 16, I was raped and beaten by an acquaintance. The fact that I felt responsible for what happened led me to keep the incident a secret from my family. I had accepted this young man's rides home, and his friendship. The friends I did tell echoed my feelings of responsibility and shame. This taught me at an early age an unspoken rule of society: Black girls and women don't matter.

Following the rape, there was no outcry of rage in the community. My father was away from us working in another time zone. Worlds away. I had no brothers to run to, and the thought of calling the police never entered my mind. The following day, I got up, got dressed, and moved on.

I moved on when I couldn't sleep at night. I moved on when I cried every time I was alone. I moved on when I was always angry, and didn't know why. And I moved on when my period didn't come. I moved on to the abortion clinic at 8 weeks. And I moved on into the arms of a much older man, thrusting me further into a world that did not nurture a young black girl in pain.

The next few years were spent in fear, anger, and loneliness. Unable to verbalize my pain, I continued to do what black women were taught from the slave ships to the boardroom harassment, backstabbing, and betrayal: Move On.

When you are trying to heal, you will make many mistakes on the road to recovery. When you need to heal but don't know it, you will continue to repeat the mistakes of the past until you hit rock bottom, and become desperate for another way. As my high school years came to a close, I became desperate for another way. Poetry saved me. Writing and reading it helped to heal me, somewhat. By the time I was on my way to college, I was determined to heal, grow, and change.

College offered me a new life. I began to open up more and make friends. I stopped being afraid of being alone with men. At school, I met young men from all over the United States who were kind, respectful, and slowly, but surely, I made platonic male friends who would walk me across campus at night, hold doors open for me, and ban together to protect us whenever violence reared its ugly head. For all intents and purposes, I was growing.

I left school and began working and reading my poetry at local open mics. I enjoyed and reveled in my femininity and independence. I maintained platonic friendships with other male poets and co-workers. Life stepped in. Then, I married a man I had become great friends with. I married him for all the wrong reasons and it didn't last.

Before the ink was dry on my divorce papers, I was in another relationship. It was my first relationship where we talked things out and settled our differences harmoniously. With him, I began to unpack years of baggage, as well as the pain of my failed marriage. We talked and listened to each other. Until then, I had begun to accept the fact that disagreements could lead to some form of abuse. What I did not understand then, that I know now, is because I was not completely healed from my past, I carried that fear, anger, and hurt into every exchange I had with people. By the time dishonesty was discovered, and my heart was broken two years later, I was beginning to figure it out.

My relationship ended with my significant other because he was in another relationship that produced a child. He didn't disclose this information to me, which made me question the authenticity of the whole relationship. To add insult to injury, the young lady was everything I wasn't. She had money, real, long hair, she was slim, and she had the man I thought I loved.

The realization brought all my insecurities and unresolved issues to the surface. I started to drown in a river of low self-esteem. My pity party brought me back to the same old way of thinking. I had not moved on after all.

I locked myself in a celibate world of anger. Every time a man was mentioned my eyes rolled. If one approached me while I was out and about, the look on my face alone would send him running. When friends and associates married and had children, I was happy for them, but believed I wasn't good enough for it to happen to me. Then, I joined a church. I began to pray and study the bible. I read self-help books, searched myself a lot, and cried a lot. It didn't happen all at once, but as time went on, I felt free.

Before I could forgive anyone, I had to forgive myself. I wrote letters to my unborn child and asked for forgiveness. And I forgave the man who attacked me. The more I fell in love with Jesus, the more I let go. My former husband and I forgave each other. Within about a week of that experience, I ran into the man I planned to marry following my divorce. By this time, he was married, and surprisingly, I was no longer mad at him! We wished one another God's best. This time, I moved on.

When you're picking up the pieces of your life, you can't move too fast. I had identified one of my issues was getting into relationships too quickly. Being alone was new for me and hard. When nobody else is around, you can truly see who you are.

Though I had made some major changes, my insides still needed a tune up every now and then. In a lot of ways, I was still a scared young girl looking for a man to protect her. I learned to protect myself. Prayer became my weapon of choice, and I saw God work miraculously on my behalf.

Still, like the Israelites in the bible who had everything, yet demanded a king, I kept asking God, "why not me?" after attending wedding after wedding.

God answered me as only He can. The Holy Spirit reminded me I was never alone. Here I was asking God for a husband, when

HE was my husband! And He sent physical representatives every day! I was reminded of all the times God sent a man to help me.

Once, in Richmond, Virginia, my mother and I went to a seafood buffet for crab legs. I was standing at the table sorting through tons of skinny, unacceptable crabs when a man tapped me on my shoulder and asked if I'd allow him to fix my plate. He returned to our table with a plate full of big, juicy crabs, lemons, extra butter, and napkins!

Another time, it was freezing cold outside, and all the tires on my car needed air. Before I could start on the first tire, a man drove up to help.

Almost daily, a man would give me a compliment, hold the door for me, or offer assistance with grocery bags. Though I don't always accept or need it, it's there.

What I have learned on this journey of self-acceptance and healing is God always gives us what we need when we need it. I'm convinced today that the vast majority of men are good. What's more, I like men. And I understand that you don't have to be against men to be for the empowerment of women. Today, I'm single, and I have and embraced my five-minute husbands!

If you look around, you will see you have some too. Embrace them, as I do, and let them give you hope for the future.

About
Marchet Denise Fullum

Marchet Denise Fullum is a mother, author, speaker, vlogger, life encourager, survivor, and tropical church girl that was raised in Mililani, Hawaii. At a very young age Marchet used writing as a form to communicate her inner most hurts, questions and thoughts. She wrote in journals to jot down her thoughts and cataloged each thought by chapters in her mind. Post-It Notes and saved computer documents eventually became the blueprint of the ups and downs of her church girl experiences. In 2016 Marchet finally decided to take elements from her journals, Post-It Notes, and saved computer documents to publish her first book, The Confessions of Church Girls. The Confessions of Church Girls is a transparent and necessary glimpse into the realities we face inside and outside the church walls.

Marchet holds a Master of Business Administration, a Bachelor of Science in Fashion Merchandising, and is a Commissioned Notary for the State of Hawaii. She enjoys consulting businesses and helping them overall to be improved from the inside out. As well as, doing interior design to help others effectively love the spaces they dwell in. Marchet also mentors young adults and teens to help them navigate through life. It is Marchet's desire to help women and men realize they are **d**estined, **e**quipped, **u**nique, **c**apable, **e**nough, and **s**trong. So, they too can put up the **deuces** and run away from everything that seeks to destroy the very essence of who they really are.

Marchet's first book, "The Confessions Of Church Girls" can be purchased on Amazon. You can email theconfessionsofchurchgirls@gmail.com for additional information.

Instagram is @thefaithfulfew

Twitter is @thefaithfulfew

No More Wire Hangers
by: Marchet Denise Fullum

"Our deepest fear is not that we are inadequate, our deepest fear is that we are powerful beyond measure. It is our light, not our darkness that most frightens us. We ask ourselves, "Who am I to be brilliant, gorgeous, talented and fabulous? Actually, who are you not to be? You are a child of God. Your playing small does not serve the world. There is nothing enlightened about shrinking, so other people will not feel insecure around you. We are all meant to shine, as children do. We were born to make manifest the glory of God that is within us. It is not just in some of us; it's in everyone. And as we let our own light shine, we unconsciously give other people permission to do the same. As we are liberated from our fear, our presence automatically liberates others."-Marianne Williamson

At a very young age I learned the many uses of a wire hanger and mastered the ability to think quick on my feet. The yells of anguish and the abuse I could hear through my locked bedroom door fueled my desire to figure out how I was going to escape. I couldn't bare to hear my mother hurting any longer as the abuser beat her with the hands that should have been loving her. Then something must have clicked in my young brain prompting my attention to the wire hangers that were strategically displaying each of my pretty dresses in my closet. I have vivid memories of me taking one of the wire hangers that held one of my pretty dresses and untangling the top of it. My hope was to utilize this untangled wire hanger so I could go rescue my hurting mother.

I removed my pretty dress from the wire hanger and I began to untangle the wire hanger as if this was a normal thing for a 2 or 3-year old to do. Now looking back as an adult, it baffles my mind that at that young of an age I was able to figure out that an untangled wire hanger could fit in the small circular door hole of my locked bedroom. It makes me ponder the possibility that although my memory picks up at this specific moment that it may not have been the first time my mother's abuser intentionally locked me behind my bedroom door. Can you imagine being surrounded by 4 four white walls that couldn't mute the cries of your mother? Can you begin to estimate how many times this occurred before I finally figured out how to escape? Is a 2 or 3-year-old little girl really supposed to successfully master the art of escape and the tactical rescue of her mother? These among many other questions have entered my mind as an adult. For the vivid accounts, I remember were the reality that my mother and I endured.

Though I remember the ugliness of my mother's abuser so clearly as if it was yesterday. I can't remember anything else from being a little 2 and 3-year-old girl on a military base in Kentucky. I have not a single memory of swinging on a swing, going to a park, eating something delicious, singing a song, watching a cartoon, or smiling as we ate dinner together in our 2-story home. I've attempted to even remember the layout of our home, during this time period, but it's as if the other areas within our home are blacked out in my mind. The only 2 areas that are illuminated as the dominant space are my bedroom and my mother's bedroom. It is as if those two fragile years in my life had been permanently filled with the memories of my mother's abuser and all other happy memories were dumped in the recycle bin of my life. It's not as if I haven't quieted myself and closed my eyes as I fished for happier moments. Yet, when I lifted up my hopeful hook not one single memory was attached. Unfortunately, the only moments still securely attached were the same cruel and destructive memories of my mother's abuser. I've tried many times to throw those cruel and destructive memories back into the sea of forgetfulness but somehow, they have remained with me throughout my journey.

As a child, it's natural to adore your mother and to have a bond that is unlike any other. For you dwelled within her as you were being formed. Formed in a temporary living area (a.k.a. your mother's womb) that protected you and provided all your daily nutrients. If I allow my imagination to chime in I believe that at a certain point within our mother's womb our hearts synced and began to beat at the same time. Her voice provided the lyrics that soothed you during this process and her laugh gave you a preview of what true joy sounded like. It was evident from day one that the responsibility that lied within her new title of "mother" was even being strengthened while you dwelled in her womb. You couldn't help but feel protected as this natural bond was leading to the day of your grand entrance. No child enters this world initially thinking they will have to provide a safe dwelling place for their mother or help to protect her. Yet, due to this undeniable bond if an abuser presents himself your instincts kick in and your roles become immediately reversed. As a child you don't sign up to master the art of escape from your intentionally locked bedroom nor do you sign up to become the top person in charge of the tactical rescue of your mother. Yet, at the sensitive age of 2 and 3 my instincts were forced to kick in and our roles were immediately reversed.

As my mother, the woman I adored, was being beaten by her abuser I was self-teaching myself to become her rescuer. No child should have to self-teach themselves how to rescue their mother from the hands of her abuser. You shouldn't also have to become a Special Ops Unit that knocks down doors and ignores all fears to jump on the back of the abuser who beats your mother as he sees fit. Yet, that was the painful reality of my 2 and 3-year-old story. The collection of visual videos I have stored within the corridors of my mind contain vivid recollections of the many times I was armed with an untangled wire hanger and tackled my mother's abuser. I didn't have the opportunity to sign myself up for a karate or a self-defense class of some sorts. I just knew that I was the only other person in that 2-story home and no one else could respond to my mother's cries. I knew in those moments it was up to me to roll out the master plan, implement it, and rescue my beautiful mother.

Therefore, I had no other choice but to put the untangled wire hanger inside my bedroom doorknob hole. I learned that the trick was to gently press the inside of the bedroom doorknob, with the untangled wire hanger, so my locked door would then open. A door that was intentionally locked each time by my mother's abusers before he went to leave his mark on my mother. I don't remember him every uttering any words before he locked my bedroom door. I just remember knowing I was locked in and I needed the cries of mother to cease. As I visualize him today he had no distinguishing mark or visual attributes that would identify him as an abuser. In fact, the average person that saw him in the neighborhood, or worked with him, or met him through one of my mother's military functions had no signs of the viscous ways this abuser utilized his hands at night. They had no way of knowing the extent of bruises and marks this abuser left on my mother's body. They didn't know that this abusers smile was deceitful and his charm was short lasting as anger consumed him. This abuser chose my mother's body as his punching bag and my mind, ears, heart, and eyes were digesting each painful blow.

Each time I successfully opened the door I would run across the hall and into the war zone. This war zone was also known as my mother's bedroom. As I entered the "war zone" I often leaped on this abuser's back as he was choking my mother or raising his hand for another brutal hit. At the time, I couldn't have been no more than 20 lbs. yet in that moment it didn't even matter to me. What mattered was for my mother's pain, suffering, cries, and yells to cease and for this abuser to quickly evacuate the premises. You would think my 20lb presence would cause his hands to cease from the brutal affliction he was orchestrating on my mother's fragile caramel body. Yet, this abuser was determined to get more smacks, chokes, and punches in with no regard that my delicate body had leaped on his back. Almost 40 plus years later I still remember the stunned look on his face every time I successfully made it into the war zone he had hatefully created. I guess this abuser thought by locking me into my bedroom I would just stay within the converted confinement. A converted confinement that seemed to exemplify the yells and cries of my mother. However, what this abuser failed to realize was the love I had for my mother caused my young mind to rapidly click for possible ways to escape. For at the age of 2 and 3 years old I knew my escape was necessary for his abuse, this time, to stop.

I couldn't have realized at that young age the impact his abuse would have in my life. For in my mind and in the foundation of my definition of men were the vivid recollections and visual videos of his cold-hearted abuse. The reality of this abuser's attacks on my mother's life played out in the corridors of my mind way before reality television debuted on our televisions. Though his abuse wasn't supposed to be absorbed as normal my young innocent mind had no other sphere of reference. So oddly enough I filed it in my mind as a normal occurrence in relationships and marriages. I witnessed first-hand the viscious cycle of abuse, then apologies, then accepting the apologies, then the love like moments, that went right back to abuse. Most people reading this would automatically assume that because I witnessed my mother being abused at a very young age that I of course would never allow abuse, of any form, to happen to me. Right? Wrong!

I'm often dumbfounded as I begin to sort through the layers of my life thus far. Even while writing this I found myself having to do it in small doses for the experience of it was the equivalent of doses of Organic Apple Cider Vinegar. It was hard to swallow and even harder as I imagined I must digest it. However, I kept on typing with a sincere hope one person's life would be impacted by my transparency. Also, knowing that each small dose would be good for me as well. So, I continued to sort and finally deal with what has been dealing with me. I'm learning that sorting through the layers of my own life does not only have the potential to impact someone else's life but without a doubt will impact my own life first. It's easy to chime in on a Domestic Violence conversation or to assist someone else as they escape a life filled with unnecessary and oftentimes reoccurring abuse. The hard work begins when we finally decide to begin to sort through our own life and begin to address the patterns that have left different marks on our life.

For me the marks have become undeniably visible as I stroll through the chapters of abuse that have happened in my life. Most of them were with fine packaged men that gave no initial signs that they were incapable of loving me but proved they could leave their mark of abuse. I started to almost accept that only a certain type of man enters my life. For as I paused and looked back it seemed as if they all had very similar threads that stitched the definitions of who they were in my life. I'm not sure if it was initially my fairytale desire to just be loved in general. It could have also been my conditioned ability to see the potential in someone while completely disregarding who they were really showing me. I didn't want to see the patterns and I definitely didn't want to acknowledge the marks. I've wrestled with the fact that when my own self-esteem wasn't where it should be a fine man could enter my life and realign my esteem to benefit his personal agenda. His abuse was coordinated through an outright attempt to dismantle and control me. The patterns that are within my life are undeniable and the marks that occurred were not just delivered by the hands of my abusers. The first patterns and marks were left at the ages of 2 and 3-years old. My mother's abuser stitched a pattern and left marks that resurfaced in my adult life. My mother's abusers attempt to control me was displayed each time he locked me in my bedroom. The impact of my mother's abuser was longer lasting than the visual evidence on my physical shell but was readily available every time I chose to hit the play button in my mind. He was the first man that attempted to control me and the first man to regularly show me a distorted version of love.

So, I found myself allowing distorted love into my adult life. As I took on the role of a rescuer in all my relationships with the men in my life. I had carried the attributes I learned from rescuing my mother from her abuser to somehow rescuing undeserving men. Men that would verbally dismantle me and men that created converted confinements similar to the one I experienced at the delicate ages of 2 and 3-years old. I learned to always put what I needed on the back burner and to make sure that I was taking care of the abuser in my life. I learned at age 2 and 3-years old, that love hurts you, love apologizes, you forgive love, and you start over again even if love came in the form of my own abuser.

Like many I was unable to initially identify my own abuser as an abuser. The entire time we were dating his package appeared to be incredible. He was kind, nurturing, thoughtful, funny, and even encouraging. Literally, from the first day we started dating not one single day went by that we didn't see each other or talk on the phone multiple times a day. We watched movies, laughed at jokes, danced, and ate Chinese food every single Friday. So of course, when he took the time to propose to me via a fortune cookie I said Yes. Within a couple of months, we were married at the good ole Justice of the Peace. Little did I know that on that Friday, October 8, 2004, my life would drastically change forever and it no longer would include Chinese food. In fact, it also didn't include a reception, wedding cake, a dance with my father, a bouquet toss, or the electric slide. Not one single friend of mine was present when we got married and my mom tried to gently rescue me. As she uttered in my ear 4 or 5 times "Marsha, you don't have to do this. You can wait and have the wedding you always dreamed of." It was as if my mom who had been abused could see the evidence of abuse from my soon to be husband. What I know for sure is my mother did not want my life to be filled with pain and now knew first-hand the signs of an abuser. Her pleas were unsuccessful and I didn't realize it completely then but the converted confinement was already being built. As the isolation, the control, and the verbal abuse surfaced and the man that dated, proposed, and married me immediately began to change.

The merry go round of love hurts you, love apologizes, you forgive love, and you start over again was a ride that started early in our marriage. The words that use to uplift me were replaced with words that were viciously aimed at my self-esteem and worth. "You're fat…you're ugly…you disgust me," became the verbal lashes he threw on a regular basis. Later kisses on the neck of my fat, ugly, and disgusted body were dispensed by my husband. As I once again forgave him and accepted his sexual make up session in hopes to cover up the verbal marks he left. I became pregnant 3 times within about a 3-year time frame. 2 of 3 of them were successful pregnancies and the miscarriage of one of them added to the depression I was already living in. I felt as if I somehow failed and at that moment every negative word he every threw at me began to surface. As I began to believe the words he frequently threw that I was fat, ugly, and disgusting.

Although, I was married I still felt so alone, as he isolated himself and created a separate space within our home. This space he purposely emphasized that I was not allowed in and he started sleeping at night in this space. This was the space he used to talk to other women, watch porn, and set up his adulterous affairs. At first, I tried to down play all the signs of his adultery and outright disrespect until one day I found out my husband had chlamydia. However, when I immediately went to get tested my results came back negative and I did not have chlamydia. Hmm…the only way that can happen is if my husband is really having sex with other women and he really was. So, he cries and he apologies and although it sounded like a familiar tune I had heard so many times I stayed. Yup…I stayed because Marchet Denise Fullum loved him and I was going to rescue him even though he was hurting me. I believed that the merry go round of love hurts you, love apologizes, you forgive love, and you start over again was a ride that I could endure and I was supposed to endure it.

Fast forward I found myself in a converted confinement nicely nested in a beautiful neighborhood near Aviano Air Force Base in Italy. I was 7,732 miles away from home. I was a military spouse, with 2 young daughters, and the only language I knew how to speak was English. This worked perfectly fine in Hawaii but in Italy all my neighbors except for 1 home spoke Italian. We had one car that I had to ask to use and 99.9% of the time the answer was no. I was a grown woman who was afraid to just take the car keys and go to the store with my daughters. He threatens to call the Italian police on me and tell them I stole his vehicle since everything was in his name. I didn't even have keys to our mailbox on base and as an adult I had to wait for him to give me my mail (and that was only if he decided to). Within 6 days of being in Italy I found out my husband was again having an affair with a female airman he met in Korea. Instead of apologizing he immediately began to remind me that I was fat, ugly, and disgusting. Honestly, at that point I didn't really feel like living any more. I didn't have keys to the car. I didn't have keys to the mailbox. I didn't have keys to my husband's heart.

I didn't want to commit suicide but I just wanted to go to sleep at night and not wake up in the morning. I know I am not the only one that can relate to feeling so overwhelmed, so restricted, so controlled, so disrespected, so verbally abused, so tired, so emotionally drained, so heavy, so weighed down, so disappointed, so manipulated, so frustrated, so disappointed, so unloved, so over it that you wonder if this is how it really is supposed to be. For me I remember feeling all of that and so much more all at one time. I literally would wake up and just pray to get through the day one second at a time. Then one second at a time led to one minute at a time. One minute at a time led to one hour at a time. Then one hour at a time led to one day at a time.

I truly believe it was the sincere prayers of others, when I felt like I couldn't pray for myself, that kept me. Along with my willingness to take it one second, one minute, one hour, or one day at a time.

Now instead of untangling hangers to unlock doors, like I did at the age of 2 and 3-years old, I made up my mind to untangle and work through what has occurred in my life. I acknowledged that I needed to get to the root of the matter so I could unlock some doors in my life and really start living. I needed to destroy some lies that were integrated, from a young age, into what I considered to be true. Then I needed to replace those lies with the facts of the matter. The facts were that I am enough, I am capable, I am intelligent, I am beautiful, I am articulate, I am lovable, I am an overcomer, and I am destined for greatness.

The key is that we have to continue to share our stories whenever we get the opportunity to. Some of our stories go beyond a handful of pages. I would be lying to you if I told you that every day has been easy. There are days that I cry as I am getting down to the nitty gritty and dealing with the foundation of where it all began. I know this is so essential because sometimes if we're not careful we will forget the importance of the foundation in our lives. We fail to realize the impact those foundations will have on our lives and the lives of others. If we don't digest that we can go back in our lives and make the necessary repairs to our foundations we will continue to live a life that is less than what we deserve. What I know for sure is that it's healthy to do regular checks on your foundation to defy the lies that you were not built to last.

I witnessed my mother getting abused at the age of 2 or 3-years old. I untangled wire hangers to insert them into a circular hole on my door knob so I could open the door. I ran across the hallway to jump on the back of my mother's abuser so I could rescue my mom. I said I do to a man that was incapable of loving me. I endured 11 years of verbal abuse by my husband who vowed to love me. His love was distorted and the cycle of control almost dismantled me. Yet, today I'm standing and transparently sharing my story with the hopes that one woman will know you don't have to stay and endure any longer. Will it be completely easy? No.! Can you do it? Of course, you can because you were built to last! My prayer for you is that you take the time to look around and identify the wire hangers in your life. Sometimes you got to use what you got to get out and face your deepest fears!

About
Kim PossABLE

As a Pittsburgh native, KimPossABLE decided to embrace the Big Apple in the early 90's, beginning with an internship at Warner Brothers Records. While working her way up the ranks, she rubbed elbows with music industry giants like Tyrese, Vanessa Williams, Biggie Smalls, Brian McKnight, Ice T, and many more. However, it was her celebrity based catering business that activated her love for events. KimPossABLE began her business catering to top record labels.

KP went on to work for a media entertainment group, marketing artists, and coordinating celebrity-based events as an Event Coordinator. Currently KP is the Project Manager for the "BLITZ" annual showcase event, the industry's largest urban music showcase, hosting artists such as: Alicia Keys, Jordin Sparks, Robin Thicke, P.Diddy, T.I., Alessia Cara, Nelly, Usher, Ciara, Janelle Monae, Rita Ora, Timbaland, K.Michelle and the list goes on. KimPossABLE is also the Producer and Host of OFF-N-RUNNING, an all access behind the scenes reality show, that gives viewers a real look into the lifestyles of its VIP guest. The show highlights **their story** while giving them a platform to showcase their vision, goals, and initiatives.

KimPossABLE is the Chief Visionary Officer of Fitzpatrick Marketing Group; a mobile marketing company based in Pittsburgh, Pennsylvania. KP continues to build her network and grow her brand by using her access, influence, and industry experience.

Emerging Spirit
by Kim PossABLE

> *"Impossible is just an opinion"*
>
> ~ Muhammad Ali

The dictionary describes the word **journey** *as an act of traveling from one place to another.*

I can truly tell you, that I'm in a very different place today, than I was three years ago

That is, before I was plucked out of my comfortable little "hiding" space

and lovingly placed on the path to my own spiritual **awakening**,.

and although it seems like a lifetime ago,

I can still recall how lonely, restricting, and painful that space was.

you know, that lonely place we go to hide out from *ourselves* and the world.

That place we go, where we get to just *coast* through life without much effort,

in a state of mere *existence,*

with no *real* sense of purpose or direction.

I, had somehow become complacent *without even realizing it,*

and without thought *or* resistance I had *voluntarily* settled into a relationship with fear.

I guess, I had become accustomed to it's hold over me...my thoughts, my actions and life.

As a result, *I lost myself.*

Awakening---awakening is an act or moment of becoming suddenly *aware* of something.

On April 7th, 2014, I **Awakened** to a voice directing me to "Step out of my comfort zone, and into a new life built on **faith** and not on fear." That same voice also **assured** me that the life I had been praying for did exist…on the other side of **fear**.

The only thing I had to do was find the courage to step out there on **faith.**

But, hadn't I done that already? The answer was *no.*

But, how could that be? When I think back to my childhood (beginning around the age of 5 years old)

I vividly remember having silent conversations with who I have now come to know to be *Jesus.*

However, at the time, I thought was just my imaginary friend.

Only to realize now, that my "imaginary friend" wasnt imaginary after all.

Needless to say, for all intents and purposes, I became a "Believer" at a very young age.

So, how could it be that I was just waking up to the *real* meaning of **faith**, *our connection to it* and the vital role it plays in our everyday lives.

It turns out, what I had done all these years was *proudly* carry my **faith** around

as if it were some sort of *glorious* gold ribbon or *badge of honor.*

Not realizing that the reason I was not living the life I imagined for myself was simply because I had never truly *activated* my **faith**. I had not put any *real* action into motion

behind my *so called* **faith.** Allow me to explain,

it's like having a platinum credit card in your wallet

but, you never took the time to call that 1-800 number on the front sticker to activate it

So it is of no use to you until you do, you can go around talking about it and flashing it all you want to, but it means nothing until you make that call.

The reality was, the *only* thing that was *ever* keeping me from becoming the person

I was created to be and *living* the life I had always dreamed of, *was me?*

Which I have to say, at the time came as a pretty hard blow to my spirit

considering I have always prided myself on having such a strong belief and **faith.**

Talk about a *rude awakening!* to say the least, I was confused.

How could what I had thought to have been **faith**, not really be faith at all?

Not in the true sense anyway. The **truth** that I was given in that moment, is that

"faith and fear could not be greater opposites!" "Faith and fear, cannot exist together."

To have **faith,** means that you believe! Without any hesitation, pause or delay.

The truth that we need to understand, is that the two *can not,* and *will not*

co-exist at the same time in the same place.   So three years, 3 months, and 17 days ago,

my **journey** to *"unbecoming"* everything that I had become, began.

The definition of the word **emerging,** is *to move out of or away from something and come into view.* Later, on my quest for a better understanding, I was led to dig a little deeper and look up synonyms for the words *emerge* and *emerging*. Below, I have shared that list of synonyms in hopes of you gaining a greater understanding and *connection with yourself.* (as I did)

<u>synonyms for **EMERGING**</u>
- Come out
- Appear
- come into view
- become visible
- Surface
- Materialize
- **manifest oneself**
- come forth become apparent , important, or prominent.

When I reviewed this list the first time, I read it over and over again.

I pondered over each and every word, as if, it were the **life-sustaining** air

that I relied on to breath. In my mind, I could hear the late Maya Angelou's poem *Still I Rise* echoing against every negative thing, that had ever happened to me and around me.

On the 10th day, of July 2011, I sat down with my journal and my favorite pen and *my spirit began to emerge.....*

<u>**My Emerging Spirit**</u>

(BE-ing free)

a **SPIRIT,**

So strong, I became weak. from the burdens I carried, constantly draining the **Life** out of me! I was **Empowering, Encouraging**, and even **Inspiring,** but not participating. I was **Smiling,** I was **Laughing,** and **Singing,** but never truly **Dancing!** I was **Trying, Crying,** and **Dying** inside, while **Lying** to myself! I'm **Focusing.** I've been **Praying.** I'm **Changing,** I'm becoming more of myself! Now I'm **Flying!** I'm **Soaring!** And in all ways I am **Roaring!** I'm even **More-ing!**

Now I'm **Saying** more! **Praying** more! I'm even **Conveying** more! I'm **Doing** more!

Wanting more! I'm shaking things up for sure! I'm **Showing** more! **Knowing** more! **Giving** and **Receiving** more! I'm making things happen more! I'm **Climbing** to my Peak, while **Creating** lots of heat, while **Moving** through all of life's defeats! I'm **Running** now, as if I'm wearing cleats, so keep up! Look At Me Now! Do you see, that the **Light** in the dark, has always been me! And when you look even Closer still, you have to believe, **God is real!!!**

Original Poem: Written by Kimberly Fitzpatrick, on the 10th day, of July 2011

When I began the process of writing, I remember being stuck *in my mind* for days.

I remember struggling with "where do I start?" Trying to figure out "what do I talk about?"

"How much do I share?" I sat in front of the computer screen staring blankly at the keys

with so much of my story swirling around in my head, all of my struggles, all the pain,

all the setbacks and set ups, at the hands of people I had loved and trusted.

I can still recall feelings of hurt, heartbreak, and loneliness. Feelings of disappointment and guilt, the losses I suffered, the mistakes I've made, the immense feelings of emptiness, that you think you'll never get over (*but, you do*) I think about all the scary times, and all the very *weary* times that I somehow managed to get through. I thought about all the tears I cried when no one else was around, and I can still recall that all too familiar *overwhelming* sense of defeat we all get. I thought about, how it feels to always be misunderstood by everyone around you especially, friends and family who, by their very connection to you, are supposed to know *who* you are. I thought about the mental, emotional, and sometimes physical abuse that I had endured over time from family members, friends, and lovers.

I reflected on the chaos, the confusion, and the dysfunction that became *"my normal."* Gratefully, these damaging experiences were also mixed with periods of good times, fun times, happiness, laughter, excitement and special moments that I will carry with me in my heart forever. And then there is the bittersweet, and all too *glorious* event that took place the 21st day of May 2003---**the birth of my son.** Which proved to be one of the most life altering events to take place thus far. For it, gave me a reason to **live,** to **fight** and to **love!** *Forever* changing the way I viewed life, death and *everything* in between.

What is **Life?** It is existence, being, and **living**. The period between the *birth* and the *death* of a living thing. In an effort to organize my thoughts, and get my story from my mind into words and ultimately to the page. I reached out to Dr. Tamika for guidance. Under her coaching I was able to gain a sense of direction and clarity. She asked---Who are you writing to? Who is your target audience? What do you want people to know? And, how do you want to leave your reader feeling?

As I allowed those questions to ping off the satellite in my brain---The answers actually began to come to mind effortlessly. *Who am I writing to?* Anyone wishing to *free* themselves from the blocks we have somehow subconsciously placed upon ourselves and our lives based on all the lies and half truths, we have been told over the years from people that either *cannot* or *choose* not to recognize and acknowledge our true power, purpose or position as it relates to assuming our rightful place in the world in which we were **created.** (Including the lies we tell ourselves)

Who is my target audience? Those *hoping* to become *free* from anyone or anything that is preventing them from being their *truest* self, and living the life they were destined for.

What do I want people to know? Know that **nothing** is impossible!

As the legendary icon Audrey Hepburn once said. *"Nothing is impossible, the word itself says **I'm possible!**"* And lastly, *How do I want my reader to walk away feeling?* My answer is this,

"Full of hope, inspired, and motivated to take action, believing that nothing is impossible!"

To begin, I would love to start my story by walking you through all of the wonderful and *miraculous* blessings that have taken place in my life this far. I want to share with you all of the positive changes that I have made not only in my life but, also *within myself*, that have since catapulted me to levels that I only dared to dream about in the past. It takes **courage** to be transparent. **Emerging Spirit** is about the power and perseverance of the *human spirit*.

Who is Kim PossABLE?

To first answer that question. I would have to tell you about Kimberly Fitzpatrick. Because, It is essential to be conscious of our past, so we don't repeat it. *Kimberly Fitzpatrick* was born October 1, 1964 in Pittsburgh, Pennsylvania. And although, she was a sickly child *(due to the lung disease asthma)* I would like to think **she was full of hope.** Although it feels like a lifetime ago, I can still recall lots happy times, exciting times, fun times playing with my siblings, family vacations, childhood friends, building barbie doll houses out of album covers, and then designing them with whatever I could find to create that dream house look. *I had dreams of being a famous interior designer* in high demand, being flown all over the country to decorate the homes of all the top celebrities. *I remember* my pet husky *chubby,* our white cat *snowball,* climbing trees and picking berries in our yard, sliding down our steep driveway on snowy days, and earning money babysitting for my Mom's friends. *I remember* walking home from school, and my favorite teacher Mrs. Smith . But, I also, remember getting picked on by the school bully, the frequent asthma attacks that would always land me in the hospital. *I remember* being so embarrassed by the eczema that would break out on my hands, so bad that I would walk around in the summertime, wearing gloves to cover them up for fear of people thinking I had leprosy, or better yet something worse. *I remember* all the loud arguments and fights in the middle of the night that would go on between my Mother and Stepfather, and how my siblings and I would hide underneath the blankets putting our hands over our ears, as if that would somehow make it all stop. *I recall* the sounds of glass breaking, from the time one of their fights got so heated, my Mom picked up a stool *(from the beautiful bar she had built, with her own hands, and covered it with this really cool blue fur)* and hurled it right out of the huge living room window, that looked out onto the front of our house! Our friends and neighbors were all asking questions the next day, that we were too embarrassed to answer, about what happened to our front window. *I remember,* when my brother got hit by a car and *(forgetting that I had asthma)* I ran 10 blocks and up two hills, all the way home to get my mother. *I remember,* my Great-Grandmother coming to live with us, and all of the conversations her and I used to have *(all the other kids were afraid of her because she was old, but not me)* I loved to pick her brain, and I would sit fixated for what seemed like hours while she shared stories about our family tree and history. One story, I never got tired of hearing was about her Grandfather, the *Cherokee Indian chief* and how our family name *Clegg*, stood for **"Proud Shoes."** I remember waking up to the flashing lights of the ambulance that came early one morning *(the sun hadn't even come up yet)* and my Mom, through tears telling us that Grandma

Clegg had passed away that night sitting up in the chair next to her bed. I think that was my first real experience with death.--- What I remember most about it , is that *it leaves you with a deep feeling of emptiness.* Of all the many conversations I had with her during that short time she stayed with us, there is one conversation in particular that I have never forgotten. One day, *she took my hands in hers* and as she rubbed her fingers over them, she stared down at my hands *as if, she was looking through to my soul and could see things that I could not possibly at that young age.* She said in a voice that I wish I could recall, *"you have wise hands, you have the hands of an old woman, that means you are wise beyond your years".*

As I stared at my hands, in an attempt to see what she was saying. I realized that although, there were a great amount of years between us, aside from my hands being a few shades lighter, *they greatly resembled hers.*

Wisdom, is one of those qualities that's hard to explain. *Are we born with wisdom?* Or is it one of those things that grows as you do? At some point, I don't recall when, I gave up my childhood dream of becoming a famous interior designer. I'm not really sure why? But, it could be because of all of the times I was told how it was an unrealistic goal, that I should focus on something more practical, something more attainable. To be honest with you, it was so long ago I cannot recall who the particular people were that *made me believe* that I was reaching too high, and for my sake, I was better off reaching for the low-hanging fruit *or better yet* the ones that fall to the ground and require no work at all. Fast forward, to years later, I now like to refer to those people as *"the dream killers"* And before I move on, I almost forgot to mention *(or maybe I have just become really good at burying that awful memory)* the *"not so good"* family member that came to live with us, (my Mother's, Brother's 16 year old son) that ended up molesting one of my 8 year old relatives--- and tragically, at 11 years old, I was the one who walked in on it, as it was happening. One of those god awful *"things"* that happens *all too often* in families. That *"thing"* no one wants to talk about, and if you dare bring it up *you* are somehow labeled a *troublemaker* just out to stir up drama. So, it gets swept under the rug and secretly hidden away, so everybody can continue with their **perfectly dysfunctional** life as if nothing ever happened. *Sadly enough, it's somehow easier for people to block it out and pretend it never happened.* That, experience is one that has haunted me my whole life. So, I can only imagine how much *havoc it has caused in hers. What made it worst, is the fact it was kept secret,* by the adults in the family giving the perpetrator a green light to ruin even more lives. Including his own biological daughters and his 8 year old Stepdaughter *(and those are just the ones we know about)* I have since gone through counseling and therapy off and on over the years, to address and begin to deal with a multitude of issues *(most centered around trust, and dating back to my childhood)* that were weighing heavy on my Psyche, and having a huge, negative impact on my life, in ways that I hadn't even realized. However, it wasn't until recently, while undergoing my first session of **Trauma therapy,** known as *Eye Movement, Desensitization and Reprocessing (EMDR)* that I was even made aware (for the very first time) that I had been *traumatized,* by witnessing something that horrific. Although, the perpetrator has since been killed in prison just a few months shy of his release, the cycle of destruction he left behind I'm sure will last for generations. *I hated him from the time I was 11 years old,* and that hate had to go somewhere.....

    I understand now, why it always felt like I carried the weight of the world on my shoulders. It's no wonder I stayed tired all the time and why something was always hurting on me physically. Whether it was my head, my back, my shoulders my knees, something was always hurting *(the manifestation of pain is real)* However, it seems inevitable since I had been carrying around so much *heavy baggage* for such a long time. *Fortunately for me, I learned it's okay to get help. Especially if you know you need it.*

According to the (ADAA) *Anxiety and Depression Association of America.* Anxiety disorders are the most common mental illness in the U.S., affecting 40 million adults in the United States aged 18 and older, or 18% of the population. (Source: National Institute of Mental Health) *Anxiety disorders are highly treatable yet only about one-third of those suffering receive treatment.*

Anxiety and Depression

It's not uncommon for someone with an anxiety disorder to also suffer from depression or vice versa. Nearly one-half of those diagnosed with depression are also diagnosed with an anxiety disorder. And judging from everything I read *women are twice as likely to be affected as men.*

FIGHT

(my FIGHT with depression)

I've been crying off and on for three days now. My eyes are red, and swollen. I have bags hanging under my eyes. Bags, filled with tears, waiting to pour out, and run down my face. My shirt is soaked with tears. **When I look in the mirror**, my reflection is old, my hairs turning grey. I'm always cold. Ask me, what I'm feeling? I would have to answer, with tears falling down my face, and a suffocating lump in my throat, **exhausted!** Mentally, emotionally, and physically, **exhausted!** My mind is **exhausted**, my heart is **exhausted**, my body is **exhausted!** I've been **fighting,** for so long! I have been **fighting** before I could even understand. **Fighting,** for my own existence! Constantly struggling. Struggling to **live**, struggling to **rise**. Struggling, to be heard. Struggling to **thrive,** struggling to **gain,** struggling not to be in pain. Struggling, just to be okay. Struggling *not* to get in my own way! Struggling and **fighting** to get through the day! **Fighting** just **to be me!** As I look around, I'm surrounded by rope on all sides---everyday that bell rings, signaling for me to **get back out there,** and fight another round! There is always one round, followed by another round, and another round, and another---it's overwhelming! **I'm tired!** I can't let my guard down for one minute. I have my fists held high! Do you really have to ask me why? Because, there's always another fight waiting---But, I **get back out there each day!** No matter, how Bloody, or bruised. To do the only thing I know how because, *these are my shoes!* I get bloodied, bruised, dazed, and confused. **Some rounds I win, some lose.** Some, fights are mine, others *I choose.* I'm fighting to keep my emotions in check. I'm **fighting** not to be a total wreck. I have to constantly **fight** with my body to stand. *I'm fighting daily, to become my own brand.* Fighting, for the right words to say, fighting and struggling, to **find my way.** I had to **fight,** just to get up today! I constantly pray to stay around. Despite, all the efforts to keep me down! Tears fall--- *but, I continue to answer the call.*

(*I hear cheering from the sidelines)* **"You can do it!"** --- " Finish the race!" I was born to fight. **This is my stage!** The only way I know how to release this rage! So, I give her a pat on the back, and wipe away her tears, as I lean down and whisper in her ear **"the key to winning, is Conquering fear!"** So, stand up! Catch your breath, but, **get back in the fight!** You must stay strong! Whatever doubt you're having, put it out of your mind!

Think *only* of your victories past and those yet to be won. When the clouds take over, I want you to picture the sun. **Remember the rainbow** because, no matter how far away! If you **keep on fighting,** you'll see it one day! Original Poem: Written by Kimberly Fitzpatrick On the 18th day, of June 2015

I chose to end my relationship with **depression**. I am now in a very loving, nurturing and supportive relationship with **Faith.** Thank you Jesus!!!

Once, I realized that the only thing that was holding me back was me, I could no longer hide behind anything *(including myself)* I could no longer hide behind people, situations, my circumstances, or my past.

The real truth is, the only one that can block you is you! You are your only limit! The only thing that stands between you, your hopes, your dreams and the life you imagined--is fear! We wake up everyday with the choice to live or hide. We can choose to either operate from a place of faith or fear, But, the choice really is ours! Every decision we make is based on our faith or our fears!

On November, 12th 2014, I chose to end my relationship with **fear,** Choosing **Faith** instead. My life has not been the same. Thank you Jesus!!!

F.E.A.R.

(fear less, to LIVE more)

For years, I belonged to you. You held me captive, ***trapped by a reality that only existed in my mind.*** You were my friend, I thought to the end, through thick and through thin. You pretended to love me. But, I in fact loathed You. However, we just continued to do, that thing that we do.

You said you needed me. But, how could that be? *we were always so opposite.* But, I suppose, if I were to oppose, it would have questioned your authority, your relevance, your place. You were always invading my space! I guess, you could say we had a love/hate going on. I thought, it would never end because, you were my only friend. So, you had me believe! But, now I finally realize, *you were just in my way.* Blocking the door, keeping me tied to the shore. You knew, **I wanted and needed more.** You are rotten to the Core! You're a liar, the ultimate deceiver! You even made me a believer. You call that love? At least admit, that you're nothing but a fake! I can't believe, I've wasted so much valuable time! *"Amazing Grace, how sweet the sound that saved a wretch like me I once was lost, but now I'm found T'was blind but now I see"*

I see, that you robbed me of reality! But, I'm not going to spend my time living bitter. I've grown, I'm better, I've become stronger! And **I'm free!** To finally see, that I don't need you!

You were never my friend, *all you did was hold me down!* Truth is, you are nothing but a clown. You can't be trusted, your heart is rusted, through to the core! You held me back, you continued to keep me in a state of lack! You're probably the reason why always wore black, for years, and years, through fears and tears. I want you to take one last look, cause' it's over! I'm closing the door! I don't need you anymore. **My destiny is waiting,** and it's long overdue! But, I can't blame you, I blame myself, for not being able to see with a **divine clarity**, that you've been lying to me. For years, and years, through all my tears. I know who you are! Your name is *fear*. And now, that we have formally been introduced--- I must inform you, that you can no longer take up space here!

So, you need to move on along--- **this is my life!** It's my time, and my rhyme! And *you can no longer be my friend.* This is, **officially the end!**

Original Poem: Written by Kimberly Fitzpatrick, on the 12th day, of November, 2015

synonyms for EMERGED
- Become known
- become apparent
- be revealed
- **come to light**
- come out
- turn up
- transpire
- unfold
- prove to be the case

I've spent most of my life going around claiming to be shy. Mainly because that title given to me at a very early age and I all too willingly accepted that label. But, shy and quiet are not the same thing. I now realize I had a lot to say but, at some point I just chose to be quiet because I didn't feel *my voice* had a place. I have since come to know that I was never shy…....I just lacked confidence.

I was a **SPIRIT** so strong…..

I became weak, from the burdens I carried, constantly draining the **Life** out of me. I've learned that **freedom** is a process with many layers. We are all cap**ABLE** of freeing ourselves from the things that hold us captive. **I chose to take my power back.**

I have **EMERGED!**

Kim Poss**ABLE**,

Mother, Daughter, Sister, Friend, Dreamer, Writer, Fighter, Visionary, Leader, Messenger, Business Woman, Creative, Marketing Consultant, Inspirational Speaker, Student of life, Believer, Truth Seeker, Spiritual Warrior and **Survivor**.

I am the original "IT" girl…..

it's my LIFE

it's my TIME

it's my TRUTH

it's my RHYME

it's my VOICE

and it's my CHOICE!

Through all of the trials, triumphs, obstacles and opportunities I have experienced, the most valuable lesson I am learning on *my journey* to rediscovering *my voice* is…**embrace the process!**

I am thriving in a world of **unlimited possibilities**, realizing the sky is NOT the limit it's only the view!

I am Kim Poss**ABLE,** and….. **I am FREE!**

FREE from depression,

FREE from trauma, and

FREE from self doubt…..FREE from fear.

Stay tuned, as *my story* continues to unfold in "BEYOND THESE WALLS" *living beyond our limits*

About
Jalila Poole - Lewis

Jalila Poole Lewis is an Author, Speaker, Blogger, Creative, Wife, Mother and Survivor of domestic violence. Jalila uses her experiences of survival, triumph, and self healing to inspire and uplift women who have suffered from domestic violence, toxic relationships, and a broken self image. She is passionate about helping women begin the journey towards healing. It is her belief that true healing starts within.

Jalila is dedicated to helping women heal, becoming the best version of themselves and turning their turmoil into victory which inspired her to become a contributing author to Project We Are Free. Jalila's journey towards healing and spiritual freedom ignited her creative aspiration to write her first novel debuting soon, "The Power of Three" loosely based on some real life events that have taken place in her life.

Jalila Poole is a San Francisco native who now resides in Dallas, Texas. When she is not working she enjoys devoting her time as a wife and a mother of four children who she absolutely adores. She is a huge fan of the outdoors, especially when near water, trees and sunlight.

Let Freedom Reign
by: Jalila Poole Lewis

"Let freedom reign. The sun never set on so glorious a human achievement"

~ Nelson Mandela

For a very long time I allowed my freedom to be imprisoned by the limitations of my own mind. Fear reigned supreme until I made a decision to heal, to love me in spite of my imperfections, to not fall victim to my many lessons some call mistakes and begin to be the woman that I have been called to be. For the Bible says, *"that it is not God that gives us the spirit of fear but of power and of love and of sound mind."* Letting my freedom reign meant no longer allowing the spirit of fear to reign in my life, allowing my faith in God and in myself become much bigger than fear. Letting my freedom reign is becoming fearless in my pursuit of happiness, love, joy and living life in abundance, it's feeling a bit of fear and doing it anyways. Letting my freedom reign is no longer asking anyone's permission to be my authentic self. It is fully accepting my Gods given talents and not letting anyone or anything hold me hostage to their perceptions, inequities or insecurities. It is allowing freedom to govern my every breath, thought and form of expression. It is not letting my past hold me captive, but to use it as the foundation to build my future. Letting my freedom reign is laying out my personal blue print towards freedom and doing so holding a place for someone else to do the same.

The beginning of my journey towards letting my freedom reign came in November of 2006- a few days following Thanksgiving. The last fight left visible bruising, a ring around my neck along with a huge bald spot that I was left to cover with my remaining braids. Women are often asked what made them leave, or when they decide enough is enough and makes the last escape attempt with the intention of never returning again. I do recall the moment I had made up in my mind I did not care to call another friend, close family member, or any of my secret keepers and disclose another episode of verbal and physical abuse. I realized I would either succumb to this, release what was left of my life to him, or I would have to plan a way to leave him for good. I was sick and tired of being sick and tired of my own sob stories, excuses, and failed attempts to escape my own misery, and at the same time not having a clue how I would actually leave him. I was in a very dark place, even feeling as though God had failed and forsaken me at times. Looking back, I now realize that I was never really all in – in seeking my freedom that is. There were parts of me that believed that I still loved this man, that was still protecting him while offering no love, protection for myself for the seed that we both shared together. I was consumed with the spirit of fear, self- hatred, denial, guilt a façade, and a distorted illusion of a family that didn't really exist.

It was a close family member that spoke to me in such a kind non-judgmental tone offering a place for my daughter and I to live. The thought of leaving everyone I loved, my job, my school, family, and friends was too much to fathom. However, her words … "Just come for a few weeks…, a month was soothing to my broken soul. Looking back now, those few weeks turned into months and months turned into seven years since I had fled from California to Vancouver, Washington a state I had no intentions of ever visiting let alone living.

I arrived to my apartment to gather all of my belongings before leaving. My apartment door was open and I was greeted by his painted foot prints marked all across the apartment floor, holes punched in the walls, pictures frames broken and all electronics, computers, and television completely gone. My personal belongings, jewelry, pictures, even my dirty clothes had been taken by him and all that was left in my apartment were my daughter's belongings. I did however have one outfit that so happen to be in the trunk of my car picked up earlier that week from the dry cleaners. I set out to drive in my four -door Honda Sedan with everything that I could fit into my car having very little space for my little girl. All that I had left to my name was stuffed into my car. It was time to say good bye to the sunshine state of California. I hit the road and began our journey through a very frightening winter snow storm arriving safely to Vancouver 12 hours later.

Months would soon pass and it would bring numerous calls from him, threats, frequent visits from him to my family members back home in California, along with emails, cyber bullying which included inappropriate pictures, phone numbers, and my social security number being leaked online. I guess there was a part of me that felt I knew what he was capable of doing and what to expect. This was not entirely true because being away meant I had not a clue of the extent he would go to if I did not voluntarily return. There were plenty of moments throughout my healing process that were filled with reminiscing on the good times that were so far in between but seemed to be magnified while away, phone calls I would make to him just to hear his voice, he would call my name and then I would hang up. This went on for a while until I found the strength to become present in the now, by embracing a new life in Washington that was being built from the ground up. Simply enjoying not having to worry about what time I had to be home, asking, begging and pleading to go places and coming up with scenarios in order to go somewhere. Constantly walking on eggshells and being so disconnected from my family and close friends. There were still the moments that I spent still rushing from the store, still on this time clock that no longer existed and shedding tears in the simplicity of washing clothes in peace. I went on day- by- day, week- by -week picking up the broken pieces of my life, reading my word daily, confiding with the people God had placed in my life, and listening to the heart of my soul.

I soon registered for school, went to the YMCA domestic violence groups, worked nights and took care of my baby girl the best way I could. I was beginning to embrace the peace and serenity that Vancouver, had to offer but, there were still many lessons to learn and still an entity that I had given life to and let consume me long ago…FEAR. Fear would soon re-introduce itself when my abuser began to crank call my Grandmother and threatening to do bodily harm to her if I did not return, his voice was different than before and I believed him. I was unsure of what he was capable of and from what he had described to me I knew that he had been stalking her. The fear was consuming me yet again, and I would make the choice to sacrifice myself instead of allowing for anyone else to be harmed in place of me. I set out to meet with him in California which initially seemed okay but soon turned into a complete nightmare. The end result would be me again being physically abused and taken against my will from California to Las Vegas. It had only been about nine months since I had been away and I didn't realized how much I had grown. I no longer fit in his world and that was very apparent to me. I was trying to figure out a plan, a way to escape again with my daughter but I was unable. I had a life now back in Vancouver, an apartment, a job, and I was almost done with school. I eventually convinced him that I would have to return back home however he would not let my daughter go. I was torn with the decision to stay where I no longer fit, suffocate and return back to both my physical, spiritual and mental imprisonment or leave so that I can continue on my path to freedom and figure out a way to get my daughter back. I gave him whatever information I needed to in order for him to go along with the plan. I told my daughter that I would return to her and that she would just be there visiting for a short time.

I had never left my daughter prior to this for more than a weekend if that, there are times when I regret not calling the police and having them escort me out of the home. There are parts of us – both my daughter and I that remain in Las Vegas that we may never get back. I would make one unsuccessful attempt to get her back resulting in him hiding her from me. The second attempt would be given to me with an exact date given to me in the spirit that I wrote down in my journal. On Friday, October 13th, 2007 I went to get my daughter and that Friday the 13th was a blessed day and not a cursed one. I set out on October 13th with very little money, the clothes on my back my return ticket, and a return ticket purchased by a sister friend that I had not spoken to in a very long time who had just called to catch up not knowing what events that had taken place.

The date had arrived and I arrived in Las Vegas, first stop was my daughters school. When I arrived at my daughter's school I requested a civil standby – which is the accompanying by law enforcement to ensure safety of both parties however it was refused because I didn't have any legal documentation and I was listed on any of the school records. I returned to the airport heartbroken, crying profusely debating if I should return home. I started to feel as though maybe I had heard wrong and that the promise was not going to be fulfilled. As I walked through a nearly empty airport I could see silhouettes of many people surrounding me and I knew that I was not alone I was traveling with a host of angels and ancestors who hadn't left my side. It reminded me of one of the many famous quotes written by the great Maya Angelou, *"I come as one, I stand as ten thousand"*.

I remained in the airport until close to midnight when I got a call from a close friend who said, "Do not leave without your daughter, I arranged a hotel for you to stay in and I'm working on a rental car". I left the airport and the next day I spent making calls to the courts, police department, and social services department to no avail. After numerous calls, I began to lose hope. I was then told that I would have to leave Las Vegas, to fly to California to get the legal documents I needed to bring back to Las Vegas as proof of the original order. I flew to California did what I needed to do there for a few hours and then it was back to Las Vegas.

I was now going to return to my daughters' school. Fear began to rise up again, I got out of the shower naked, immediately fell upon my Bible and cried out to God saying, I am like Moses, I do not know the words to speak. As I continued to cry out in prayer I heard a familiar voice coming from the television it was Joel Osteen saying during one of his sermons that "God was working behind the scenes on your behalf. I picked up a rental car and again headed back to my daughter's school and again called for a civil standby. God had already given me a few dreams prior to leaving to get my daughter. In one of the dreams I had arrived at her daughter's school and was directed to a room in the back after walking down a long hall and I was reunited with my daughter, I was told that an officer was on his way. I went into the school and exactly as I dreamt, I was escorted down a long hall to a small room. There I stood nervous and anxious awaiting the police officer to arrive. Then I heard the officer approach the staff, I heard a quiet voice that said, "It will appear as though he is here for them but he is here for you,", he entered the room and spoke with me briefly, I told him the story and that I had documentation from California showing the original court orders in which I was the custodial parent, and him visitation. The officer listened and then replied, "I will have to call him to give him the opportunity to show proof of a more recent order" he could see the fear in my face and reassured me that he would remain with me and I had nothing to be afraid of. He then made the call, and my stomach was torn into knots. He spoke a few words, listened and then hung up the phone. The officer gave him the opportunity to bring the documents. We waited for what seemed to be an hour, and he called again, no answer. He left a message and said if he does not come with the documentation, I could leave with my daughter. The officer began to speak in such authority, he requested the assistance of the Principal, he demanded all of my daughter's school records to be released, advised the secretary that his orders came from the high chief and to release the child to her Mother immediately. At that very moment, I thought to myself, "High chief", maybe the calls I was making to the police stations, had been documented and that indeed God was working behind the scenes on my behalf and connections were being made, maybe the high chief wasn't a chief officer but the supernatural authority of God.

I sat as I had dreamt it before in a very low chair in a small room, as my daughter entered the room, very timid, shy, and in complete shock showing little to no emotion. I stretched my arms towards her as she began to walk towards me and I embraced her. The feeling of her being in my arms was just as I had dreamt it weeks prior. My eyes filled with tears of joy and pure happiness as I held my baby in my arms after four months of her absence. I immediately called my cousin who was waiting by the phone, "I got her!", I screamed as we both cried the ugly cry I glanced at the clock with my baby in my arms. The clock read 2:52, I yelled, "it's 2:52", we continued to cry as the words couldn't even begin to penetrate. You see, what was symbolic to it being 2:52 was a testimony to Gods promises coming true, and a seed that we had sown in church months prior when an internationally, well-known visiting pastor by the name of T.D. Jakes had come to Portland, Oregon and he preached a sermon on Luke 2:52, "*And Jesus increased in wisdom and stature, and in favor with God and man*". We had sowed a seed of $252.00 dollars during that service, and we recited this scripture daily. From that day on we would see the synchronicities in this number. It was as if it followed us everywhere we went, signs and wonders they followed me.

Many miracles happened in those five days and the unseen hand of God orchestrated the events leading up to me bringing my baby back home safely. It wasn't until we were on the airplane and we began to take off, that my daughter looked at me, placed her small hand over my face and said, "Mom its really you!", I knew it was going to be a good day because today was ice cream day and God told me it was going to be a good day", and she finally embraced me fully and together we wept. I realized now that God's promises were two-fold. It had to be this day that I brought her home because I had made a promise to her as well. I learned a lot in those five days, I learned the power of prayer, sacrifice, and how having faith and holding on to God's promises even when no one else believes you.

I did not have a lot of support when I told people that God had told me to go and get my daughter on Friday the 13th, even people I considered prayer warriors, said not to go, it's too dangerous, you don't have the money, how are you going to do this by yourself. Truth is I never was by myself, I had a host of angels with ancestors and spirit guides, all under the authority of the me, ancestors, and spirit guides, all under the authority of the Great I am, the universe had conspired with me to bring forth the promises and it yielded. The same police car that was parked in front of the school when I initially made the call to the police station for a civil standby was in fact the same exact car that the officer whom was already in the building got into. There was never an officer on the way, he was already there, as spoken to me in the spirit, "he will appear to be here for them but he is here for you". That same officer escorted me to my hotel to check out, to get gas to fill up the rental car, and was on guard every step on the way assuring my safety; he escorted me outside of his jurisdiction to the airport.

Upon my arrival to the airport I stood in line anxiously waiting to get the front of the line to get my boarding pass. When I arrived to the front I gave my name, and the lady stood there with a very unnerving expression on her face, "she said, "are you in trouble ma'am?" Before I could reply she went on to say a man had came here looking for you, "he was very hostile and threatening in his tone". She continued with the transaction however unbeknownst to me she had pushed an emergency button underneath the counter and I was soon escorted by several officers throughout the airport. As I approached the top of the escalator there he stood, "exclaiming to the officers that surrounded him that he just wanted his family back, "I comforted my daughter in my arms and never looked back.

It has been 10 years since that event took place, during the course of the 10 years there have been numerous court appearances, doubts, fears, battles, and some lasting effects of Post-Traumatic Stress Disorder, counseling for both my daughter and I and a host of blessings, ups and downs and continued growth. I often look back at the events that took place during that time and all of the miracles that I witnessed during those days. For example, no police report was ever found with that officer's name; even at the request of my attorney to the Las Vegas police it is still not on record.

God's promises are indeed true, and although this part of my story is sometimes the hardest to tell I have come to realize that it was never all about me. The story had to be told, not for me, but for the women who share a similar story, suffer in silence, have lost their children both temporarily and sometimes permanently. Those who have stood before countless judges that have overlooked the symptoms of PTSD amongst victims of domestic abuse, those who don't take in to account the psychological damage that is done. Those of us in fear of retaliation didn't call the police so when we do get up the courage to finally leave we lack the proof required by the law to protect our children or ourselves. I tell my story for those who have lost sight of themselves, those unable to protect themselves let alone their children as they watch their mother being abused and for the children who fall victim to the same violence as well.

It is amazing how when you step into the unknown and the vastness of the universe with only a promise in your hand solely trusting in God, what God can truly do. I am a living witness that God can make your crooked path straight and aligned everyone on your path on your behalf to bring forth the promise. When I think back to the woman I once was a young lady who was torn down spiritually, physically, mentally and emotionally. A woman who had lost it all, forced to flee to another state and who would be hidden behind the curtain allowing God to restore her so that when the curtain was raised she would let reign free.

It would be a year or so later that my purpose would be revealed. Paulo Coelho wrote in *The Alchemist* "*To realize one's destiny is a person's only obligation*". My realization came as I sat in my car with the sun glazing against my face and the spirit spoke to me giving me a title of a book that I was to write, "*The Power of Three*", I began to see different scenes of the three women together, I was given the ending of the story and who the artist would be to draw the cover of the book. Another voice echoed in the wind as well saying, 'you don't have anything to write this on", and I spoke back to it saying, "yes I do", and I began to write the information that was being downloaded onto a receipt I found in my glove department. One of the main characters in the fiction novel is loosely based on actual events that have taken place in my life.

The Power of Three is an epic story of three women whom through their broken past form a sacred trinity, that ultimately changes their lives forever. Together, they overcome their fears; heal their innermost deepest layers while embracing the power that has been hidden within them all along. Each woman's unique story will empower you, encourage and renew your faith in sisterhood. It will challenge you to heal, be whole, and use your pain as the catalyst to build your dreams, live life abundantly -with no regrets.

I would have never envisioned myself as an author 10 years ago, as a domestic violence survivor and an advocate for women and that I would be so passionate about the innate power that women possess within.

One important spiritual law that I live by is **intent**. I believe that our intent must be poised with the greater good for humanity, to cultivate, to manifest, and bring forth healing, peace and love in abundance. It is with this in mind that I bring you my story, "Let Freedom Reign", in doing so I choose to come out of hiding to be used as a guiding light of hope for whoever reads this story. It is my hope that by sharing my story that you too will be able to let freedom reign in your life as well as in the lives of others.

Conclusion

It is our hope that you approach your life as though you are free to be whoever you need to be to live and walk in the purpose you were assigned to fulfill. Knowing who you are is the fastest path to freedom. Your seed of purpose has been planted in your soul. What you are going through or what you've gone through will sometimes awaken you to your purpose and exactly what you need to do to experience the freedoms in life that so many people long for. Every second is a chance to make a change in your life. Ask yourself what do you need to have in place for your breakthrough to happen. Stand firmly in your worth and own who you are. Most people are not confident because they don't trust themselves. Trust yourself to make the right decisions in every aspect of your life. When fear creeps in, know that fear was created by your ego to keep you safe, comfortable, and to keep you from getting to the other side of fear. Don't let fear dominate you.

The women in this book decided to face their fears with boldness and courage because they had grown tired of remaining the same in dead end, painful situations. We are here on this journey together. Feel free to contact with these women so that they can help you along your path to setting yourself free. If you don't like your situation, you have the power to change it. Take action like your life depends on it. You don't want to die with regrets. Don't take all of your gifts and ideas to the grave yard. Take action!

www.ingramcontent.com/pod-product-compliance
Lightning Source LLC
Chambersburg PA
CBHW070302230526
45470CB00002B/681